TEACH YOUR CHILDREN TO LOVE THE PROPHET

MUHAMMAD

Dr. Muhammed Abdu Yamani

DAR AL-TAQWA

© Dar Al Taqwa Ltd. 1995

ISBN   1 870582 45 4

Translation: Aisha Bewley

Editors: Abdalhaqq Bewley and Muhammad Isa Waley

Production: Bookwork, Slough.

Published by:
    Dar Al Taqwa Ltd.
    7A Melcombe Street
    Baker Street
    London NW1 6AE

Printed in Great Britain by:

Deluxe Printers
245A Acton Lane
Park Royal
London NW10 7NR

Tel: 0181-965-1771

بسم الله الرحمن الرحيم

In the name of God, most Gracious, most Merciful

Table of Contents

Chapter One
Teach Your Children to Love the Messenger of Allah
may Allah bless him and grant him peace

Loving Allah's Messenger, may Allah bless him and grant him peace

Teach your children that the Prophet Muhammad, may Allah bless him and grant him peace, was the finest of the Chosen Ones, the noblest of the Prophets, and the Seal of the Messengers. Before his mission he was known as the Truthful, the one worthy of trust; and after his mission he was the mercy given to all people. He was the answer to Abraham's prayer to his Lord, the prophecy of Moses and Jesus, and the leader of the Prophets. He was the best of all who believed in the Message. He discharged the Trust, advised the Nation (*umma*), and strove in the Cause of Allah until he passed away.

Teach them that he was more precious to the believers than their own souls, and that he was the Prophet to whom all other Prophets had pledged allegiance. He was a mortal man who received Revelation. He was the best example of all those who *"set their hopes in Allah and the Last Day, and remember Him abundantly."* (33:21)

Teach them that Allah Himself swore by *his* life, although He had not done this for any other prophet. He said: *"By your life, they were wandering blindly in their drunken state!"* (15:72)

When He addressed him, he praised him above all other Prophets and Messengers.

Sow love for him in their hearts, and for the pure and good members of his family, and remind them of his statement: "Whoever loves me, Allah will love him, and whoever hates me, Allah will abhor him." [1]

Tell them that a believer is not a true believer and cannot taste the sweetness of faith until Allah and His Messenger are dearer to him than all else.

The pages that follow are a modest contribution to the life and conduct of the Prophet Muhammad, may Allah bless him and grant him peace. They have been published in a variety of places before being collected in the present work. It is to be hoped that they will be of benefit, Allah willing, to all.

My primary motive is to encourage people, particularly parents, to give young people access to the life-story of the Prophet, may Allah bless him and grant him peace, so that it becomes a guiding light in their lives and a pattern to follow in all their affairs and so they will adhere to it in everything they do or say to the best of their abilities. For he was the best example for his Companions and for the entire nation of Islam and will continue to be so until the earth and everything upon it returns to Allah; as Almighty Allah has Himself ordained: *"There is ever a goodly example for you in the Messenger of Allah."* (33:21) The noble Prophet said: "Follow my *Sunna* and the *Sunna* of the rightly-guided Caliphs after me. Hold fast to it most fervently!"

Consequently, it is our duty to teach our families and children to love his noble and faithful Companions. We pray that Allah sow love for them and love for those who love them in our hearts, and grant us obedience to our beloved Prophet so that we may gain salvation through his Intercession, drink the water of the Basin from his noble hands, and meet him with him satisfied and pleased with us.

Many wise men have realised the importance of using great historical events as a means of attracting the interest of the young

1. Narrated by at-Tabarani in *al-Kabir*.

to the glorious heroic achievements of the Muslim community and as a method of inculcating values and ideals in their hearts. They also appreciate the educative value of a study of the *Sira*[1] of Muhammad, may Allah bless him and grant him peace, and an examination of his exalted qualities and upright manners, the majesty of his moral perfection and the greatness of his conduct in situations of every kind. He was foremost among men in providing the means to refine the younger generation's conduct, improve their intellectual faculties, and furnish them with an ideal and supreme model.

Every year, we witness the great occasion of the anniversary of the birth of the Prophet, may Allah bless him and grant him peace, which initiated a new era in the history of the world and the rise of the glory of Islam. The month of Rabi' al-Awwal arrives radiating light and a fragrance sweet and dear to our hearts. All over the world Muslims welcome this occasion with gladness and joy, reciting the Glorious Qur'an, reading and recalling the *Sira*, and remembering the Messenger's great personality and his perfect appearance and behaviour. They reflect upon the way he saved mankind from the darkness of polytheism and idolatry, and actualised humanity's dignity and integrity. They recall how heaven, earth, and all created things cheered with joy when he was born.

This occasion is a powerful motivation for the younger generation to love and venerate his law and to act earnestly in accordance with it. It is a good opportunity to gather our children every year to study the *Sira* of this noble Messenger and the way Allah endowed him with the greatest of attributes. We will then realise that his character was inspired by the Qur'an, for Allah Himself has praised him: *"Truly you are of a tremendous character."* (68:4)

---

1. *Sira*: the Prophet's sayings and way of life.

Sira Day

It is desirable for parents to sit with their children and study the *Sira* together. In fact, I believe that this is a duty for schools as well. If only they could set aside one day of Rabi' al-Awwal each year and call it "*Sira* Day" when pupils and teachers could get together without reprehensible innovations, excess, or exaggerated rituals. It should be a dignified occasion of knowledge and wisdom. It is not necessary to have it on the actual anniversary of his birthday, may Allah bless him and grant him peace. It could take place on any day during Rabi' al-Awwal, or even in some other month. The aim is to link our children to the life of our Prophet, may Allah bless him and grant him peace, from the time he was a blessed foetus in his mother's womb, the moment of his birth (when he came to the earth as if in prostration) filling the whole house with light, comfort and elegance, until he was breast-fed in the Banu Sa'd tribe.

He twice tasted the bitterness of orphanhood and later lost his grandfather but developed in such a way that even as a child he was known for his purity as he never worshipped an idol. He never joined any gathering whose purpose was idleness or immorality. His tribe, Quraysh, admitted his uniqueness and noble nature, calling him the Truthful and Trustworthy. Later, he took care of the business transactions of Khadija, who subsequently became his first wife later). During his journeys, many signs of his impending prophethood were witnessed by Maysara and other people. His dealings with the merchants in the marketplace were marked with honesty and fairness.

Later he married Khadija, one of the noblest women of Quraysh, who chose him in preference to all the nobles of Makka. She gave birth to daughters in a society that disfavoured girls and even buried its female infants alive. The Prophet was just as happy with his daughters as he was when his sons Al-Qasim and 'Abdullah were born. This was a real challenge to the pagan Quraysh who were immersed in misguidance and polytheism.

There followed a great dispute among the Qurayshite tribes over the replacement of the Black Stone during the reconstruction of the Holy Ka'ba. They were about to resort to bloodshed but were rescued from it by the wisdom and good counsel of the Truthful and Trustworthy.

Our children must become familiar with this dimension of the Prophet's great life during the Days of Ignorance preceding his Messengership. It will form a foundation for the study of other dimensions of his character after the advent of Islam.

❋❋*

His prophethood started with days of isolation and worship in the cave of Hira. Then came the great moment of revelation through the angel Gabriel: *"Read in the Name of your Lord and Cherisher Who created. He created man out of a germ cell. Read, and your Lord is the Most Bountiful. He who taught (the use of) the pen. Taught man what he did not know."* (96:1-5) From this our children will learn that their religion is a religion of learning and knowledge. The first word revealed was "Read" which links knowledge to religion and makes them inseparable. Knowledge is the basis of faith in Allah. Faith is the source of all knowledge and strengthens people's hearts. It is through faith that the believers accomplish their miracles in every field.

It is essential that our children be aware that he is the both best of and also the Seal of the Messengers. Let them listen to the Qur'anic verses and the *hadiths*, as well as the narratives of scholars and historians.

Allah Almighty made a covenant with all the Prophets and Messengers that if they were to witness Muhammad's mission, they would believe in, follow, and support him. The Prophets and Messengers in their turn took the covenant of their people after them that if they were to witness Muhammad's prophethood, they would believe in him and support him. Allah Almighty says: *"Behold! Allah took the Covenant with the Prophets, saying: 'I give you a Book and Wisdom; then shall come to you a Messenger, confirming what is with you; so believe in him and render him help.' Allah said: 'Do you agree, and take this My Covenant as binding on you?' They said: 'We agree.' He said: 'Then bear witness, and I am with you among the witnesses.'"* (3:81)

5

Muslim relates that Allah's Messenger said: "Allah has chosen Kinana from among the sons of Isma'il, and Quraysh from among Kinana. From Quraysh He has chosen the family of Hashim, and from the family of Hashim, He has chosen me."

Similarly, our children should know that the scholars of *Sira* unanimously agree that he was a descendant of Isma'il, son of Abraham, a lineage famous for generosity, high morals, courage and audacity. Both their actual deeds and their lineage proved them to be the best of mankind.

He said of himself, "I am the best of you and so are my fathers and forefathers."[1]

His name is: Muhammad ibn 'Abdullah ibn 'Abdu'l-Muttalib ibn Hashim ibn 'Abd Manaf ibn Qusayy ibn Kilab ibn Murra ibn Ka'b ibn Lu'ayy ibn Ghalib ibn Fihr ibn Malik ibn an-Nadr ibn Kinana ibn Khuzayma ibn Mudrika ibn Ilyas ibn Mudar ibn Nizar ibn Ma'ad ibn 'Adnan, of the progeny of Isma'il, son of Abraham, may Allah bless him and grant him peace.

His mother was an eminent descendant of the family of Zuhra. She was Amina bint Wahb ibn 'Abd Manaf ibn Zuhra ibn Kilab ibn Murra ibn Ka'b ibn Lu'ayy ibn Ghalib ibn Fihr.

Allah Almighty assigned prophethood to Muhammad even before he created Adam. It is related on the authority of Abu Salama that Abu Hurayra said: "The Companions once asked, 'O Messenger of Allah, when did prophethood become your necessary right?' He replied, 'When Adam was between [the state of] spirit and flesh.'"[2] He also said, may blessings and peace be upon him: "I am a slave-servant of Allah and the Seal of the Prophets, in whose nature Adam is subsumed."[3]

He was known for truthfulness, honesty and moral uprightness throughout his life. He was truly the *'mercy bestowed on the Universe.'* The Qur'an says: *"We have sent you only as a mercy to the Universe"* (21:107). Allah also said to the Prophet's people: *"A Messenger has come to you from among yourselves, grievous*

---

1. Narrated by Muslim, Chapter: The Prophet's Genealogy.

2. Narrated by at-Tirmidhi and al-Hakim and they proved that it is *'sahih"* (authentic).

3. Narrated by Ahmad and al-Hakim and they said that it is *'sahih'*. It was also classed as authentic by adh-Dhahabi.

6

to him is your suffering, who is greatly concerned for you, who is most kind and merciful to the believers" (9:9).

Among his names were: "Prophet of Mercy", "Messenger of Mercy", and "the Mercy Bestowed." Al-Hakim has related on the authority of Abu Hurayra that the Messenger of Allah, may Allah bless him and grant him peace, said: "O people, verily I am a mercy bestowed."[1]

Shaykh Abu Zahra mentions in his book, Seal of the Prophets, that the mercy which the Prophet embodied was universal, for all humanity. He says that some of his Companions said, "Messenger of Allah! You speak constantly of mercy, although we are merciful to our spouses and our children!' "That is not what I mean. I mean mercy to each and every being," he replied. He was merciful when treating sick souls and kind and compassionate when he cured those who were astray.

One day a bedouin came to ask him for something. The Prophet gave him what he wanted and asked:

"Have I been good to you?"

"No, you have not," the bedouin replied in an insulting tone. Those present were very angry at the bedouin, but the Prophet, may Allah bless him and grant him peace, told them to leave him alone. The Prophet then entered his house and called for the bedouin to give him something else.

"Have I been good to you?" he asked again.

"Yes," the man replied, "may Allah reward you on behalf of my family."

The Prophet, may Allah bless him and grant him peace, then said, "When you first spoke, my Companions were unhappy; so if you wish, tell them what you just said to me, so that their hearts feel no resentment towards you." The bedouin agreed to this proposition.

The following morning, the Prophet, may Allah bless him and grant him peace, came out and said: "The bedouin said what he said, so I gave him something more, and he claims that he is now satisfied. Is it so?"

---

1. Narrated by al-Hakim and classed as authentic by adh-Dhahabi; also narrated by at-Tabarani and al-Bazzar, as well as al-Haythami in *Majma' az-Zawa'id*; 8/257.

"Yes," the man said, "may Allah reward you on behalf of my family."

Then the Messenger of Allah, may Allah bless him and grant him peace, said, "In my dealing with this man I am like someone whose camel has run away; the more the people try to chase it, the more the camel runs away. Its owner then says, 'Leave it alone, for I am kinder to it than you and I understand it better.' So he quietly follows the camel with some fodder in his hand. The camel comes back to him and kneels down and he mounts it. If I had left you to act against the man because of what he said, and had you killed him, he would have gone to Hellfire."[1]

Similarly, the Prophet was kind to children. He used to hug them, and would allow his two grandchildren to climb on his back while he was prostrating in prayer. He used to stay for long periods in prostration so as not to disturb them. Whenever he heard a child crying while he was praying, he would shorten the prayer so that someone could go and comfort it.

A man came to the Prophet, may Allah bless him and grant him peace, and said, "I pledge allegiance to you to emigrate and perform *jihad*, seeking reward from Allah."

"Are either of your parents alive?" the Prophet asked.

"Yes, both of them," he said.

"Are you seeking reward from Allah?"

"Yes," he said.

"Then go back to your parents and be a kind companion to them," the Prophet advised.[2]

So great was his mercy that it extended to animals. He considered them more deserving of compassion than humans, in greater need of it because they cannot complain or express their grievances. 'Abdullah ibn Ja'far relates that the Prophet, may Allah bless him and grant him peace, once entered a garden belonging to one of the Ansar where he found a camel. As soon as the camel saw the Prophet, its eyes filled with tears of longing for sympathy. The Prophet went to it and put his hand on its neck in tenderness. The camel calmed down. He asked about its owner. When the man

---

1 *As-Sira*, II.72.

2. Agreed upon; this *hadith* is in Muslim's compilation.

8

came, the Prophet said to him: "Don't you fear Allah? You are mistreating this animal which Allah made subservient to you. It complained to me that you overwork it and let it starve."[1]

Our children should learn these stories, for they will instil the love of mercy in their hearts. They will love the Prophet of Mercy, and aspire to imitate him and hold fast to everything he said and did. Let us read them *Sura* 94 which begins: *"Have We not expanded your breast?"* They will understand that Allah raised him in high esteem and forgave him.

Qatada, may Allah be pleased with him, said, 'Allah exalted his memory in this world and in the next. Any orator or speaker quoting his sayings or anyone conveying a message declares, 'I bear witness that there is no deity but Allah and Muhammad is the Messenger of Allah.'" What honour could be greater than this?

Al-Qadi 'Iyad writes in his book, *ash-Shifa'*: "One sign of his unique attributes and the special favour accorded to him by Allah is the fact that Allah addresses all the Prophets by their names: 'O Adam! O Noah! O Moses! O David! O Jesus! O Zachariah! O Jonah!' But He addresses Muhammad, may Allah bless him and grant him peace: 'O Prophet! O Messenger! O enfolded in a garment! O enwrapped in a cloak!'"

Ibn al-Jawzi said: "Allah the Exalted has never sworn by the life of any other man, because in His sight Muhammad is the noblest of all humankind. He says: *'By your life'* (15: 72)."

Ibn 'Abbas said: "Allah Almighty has never created anyone nobler than our master Muhammad, may Allah bless him and grant him peace. Allah glorified him and took the Covenant with the Prophets to follow him. He says: *'Behold! Allah took the Covenant with the Prophets, saying: "I give you a Book and Wisdom; then comes to you a Messenger, confirming what is with you; so believe in him and render him help." Allah said: "Do you agree, and take this My Covenant as binding on you?" They said: "We agree." He said: "Then bear witness, and I am with you among the witnesses." If any turn back after this, they are perverted transgressors.' (3:81-82)"*

---

1. Narrated by Abu Dawud in the Book of *Jihad*.

9

Jabir, may Allah be pleased with him, narrates that the Messenger of Allah, may Allah bless him and grant him peace, said: "I have been given five things which were not given to anyone before me. I have been given victory through fear and at the distance of a month's journey. The whole earth was made a place of worship for me, so anyone of my nation can pray anywhere at the time of the prayer. Spoils of war taken in battle are lawful to me, while they were not lawful to any Prophet before me. And whereas each previous Prophet was sent to his own people, I was sent to all mankind, and I have been given the power of Intercession."[1]

Hadith scholars mention that he said: "I have been given the all-inclusive sayings and I am the Seal of the Prophets."

Allah the Exalted says: *"Muhammad is not the father of any of your men, but he is the Messenger of Allah and the Seal of the Prophets."* (33:40)

It is narrated that he said, "My community has been made the best of all communities."[2]

Our children might ask about the meaning of the Prophet's saying: "I am the prayer of Abraham." We should therefore remind them of the story of the Prophet who addressed his Lord while raising the foundations of the Holy Ka'ba with his son Isma'il. We should recite to them the following verse:

"O our Lord! And send among them a messenger from amongst themselves who will recite Your Signs to them, and teach them the Book and the Wisdom, and purify them. Truly You, only You, are the Mighty, the Wise!" (2:129)

Ibn Jarir relates on the authority of Abu'l-'Aliyya that when Abraham, upon whom be peace, said, *"O our Lord! And send among them a messenger"* he was told, "Your prayer is answered. He shall come at the end of time."[3]

Ibn Sa'd narrates that Ibn 'Abbas, may Allah be pleased with him, said, "When Abraham was commanded to take Hagar away, he was taken up on al-Buraq, and whenever he passed by some flat

---

1. Agreed upon; al-Kirmani's commentary on the *Sahih* of al-Bukhari, vol. 4, p. 97.

2 Ibn Mardawayh on the authority of Ubayy ibn Ka'b.

3. At-Tabari, *Tafsir*.

green land with running water, he asked, 'Shall I descend here, Gabriel?' But Gabriel only said, 'No,' until they reached Makka. There Gabriel told him, 'You should descend here, Abraham.' Abraham said, 'There is no agriculture or vegetation here.' Gabriel replied, 'In this place shall appear the Prophet from the offspring of your son, and by him the Highest Word shall be brought to perfection.'"[1]

Muhammad ibn Ka'b al-Quradhi, may Allah be pleased with him, once said: "When Hagar left with her son Isma'il, they met someone who said, 'O Hagar! Your son shall be the source of many nations. From his nation shall appear the Unlettered Prophet who will dwell in the sacred precincts (Makka)."[2]

Children might ask, "How was the Messenger of Allah the Imam of the Prophets?" They should be told the story of the *Isra'* and *Mi'raj* when the Prophet, may Allah bless him and grant him peace, led all the Prophets in prayer in Jerusalem on the night he was taken from the Sacred Mosque to the al-Aqsa Mosque.

He was indeed the best among the faithful and the bearer of the trust. He underwent all sorts of sufferings while spreading his message among people who were deeply rooted in ignorance and blinded by their worship of idols. He was kind in words and gentle when counselling his people. He was gentle in persuasion, neither rough nor arrogant. He was forbearing, patient, and human, as he tried every means to guide his people, using the sword only when he and his followers had been subjected to persecution and torture at the hands of the ruthless masters of Quraysh and its polytheists and idol-worshippers, who confiscated their properties, tortured people, and committed all evil acts, even murdering women and children.

Finally the Prophet's followers were forced to emigrate to Abyssinia and leave their homes and kinsmen behind. Then came the Emigration to Madina after thirteen years, when Allah gave them permission to engage in warfare. Allah says: *"To those against whom war is made permission is given to fight because they have been wronged. Verily Allah is Most Powerful for their aid."* (22:39) The Prophet emigrated from Makka for the sake of

1 Ibn Sa'd, *Tabaqat*, i, 107.

2. Ibn Sa'd, *Tabaqat*, i, 107.

his religion to the city of Yathrib which gave him a warm welcome. He changed its name to al-Madina, established the bonds of brotherhood between the Emigrants (*Muhajirun*) and Supporters (*Ansar*), and built his holy mosque. He invited people to the true faith aided by his Companions. Many hearts embraced the new religion. In al-Madina he destroyed all the citadels of idol worship. He fought three great battles: Badr, Uhud and al-Ahzab. When the misguided and deceiving Jews betrayed him and broke their bonds in disloyalty, he expelled them from al-Madina.

He established the great Islamic state as a source of guidance and manifestation of true religion. He continued his *Jihad* to spread Islam until the very last moment of his life. Even as he was dying, he prepared the army led by Usama heading for the Byzantine territories.

The Prophet Muhammad, may Allah bless him and grant him peace, had more rights over the believers than their own selves, as Allah the Exalted states: *"The Prophet is closer to the believers than their own selves."* (33:6) He was deeply concerned about the interests of humanity, sparing no effort or sacrifice whatsoever to save humankind from the punishment in this life and the Hereafter. It is appropriate in this connection to mention the *hadith* of the Prophet in which he said, "I am to you like a man who kindles a fire into which moths mindlessly keep falling. I struggle to hold you from it to save you, but you slip from my hand and fall into it."

This highly expressive image, once embedded in the children's minds, will serve as a lifelong protection for them whenever they come near the abyss of corruption that leads them to sins for which Allah will punish them in this world and the Next. Remind them that the true belief which humanity enjoys, and the perfect and complete law which brings peace, security, and an honourable life, are a favour from Allah and a result of the Prophet's effort.

It is incumbent upon people to love the Prophet Muhammad, for Allah Almighty says: *"Say: If your fathers and your sons, and your brothers and your wives and your families, and wealth which you have gained, and commerce in which you fear a failure, and houses which you love, are dearer to you than Allah and His*

Messenger, and Jihad *in His cause, then wait until Allah shall bring His command to pass. Truly Allah does not guide the people of deviance."* (9:24) He also says, *"Say: If you do love Allah then follow me: Allah will love you."* (3:31)

Al-Qadi 'Iyad comments on the former verse: "This verse is a clear proclamation and a patent proof that the love of the Prophet is an obligation and that the Prophet is worthy of that love. Allah the Exalted threatens those who love their wealth, family, and children more than Allah and His Messenger. He says: *'Then wait until Allah shall bring His command to pass.'* He declared them to be people of deviance in the last part of the verse, informing them that they are misguided and astray. Therefore, no believer enjoys true faith and its sweetness and delight in his heart unless Allah and His Messenger are more beloved to him than all else."[1]

On the authority of Anas, may Allah be pleased with him, it is related that the Prophet, may Allah bless him and grant him peace, said, "A man will taste the sweetness of faith when he finds three things in himself: that Allah and His Messenger are dearer to him than all else, that he loves his brother purely for the sake of Allah, and that he would hate to return to disbelief after Allah has rescued him from it just as he would hate to be thrown into a fire."[2]

'Amr ibn al-'As said: "No one was ever dearer to me than the Messenger of Allah, may Allah bless him and grant him peace, nor was anyone greater in my sight. So great was my respect for him that I could scarcely look at him directly, and if I were asked to describe him, I would not be able to do so."[3]

The story of Zayd ibn ad-Dathinna is a fitting example which shows how the Muslims loved the Messenger of Allah, may Allah bless him and grant him peace. Al-Bayhaqi relates that 'Urwa once said, "When the people of Makka took Zayd ibn ad-Dathinna from the Sacred Mosque to kill him as a prisoner after the battle of Raja', Abu Sufyan ibn Harb, still an idolater at that time, asked him, 'By Allah, would you be happier if Muhammad were now to be killed in your place instead of you, and I were to let you go to

---

1. Al-Qadi 'Iyad, *ash-Shifa'*, vol ii, p. 25.
2. *Riyad as-Salihin*, 178.
3. Muslim.

13

your family?' But Zayd replied, 'By Allah, I would not be happy if Muhammad were to be pricked by a thorn where he is now while I was safe and secure with my family.' Abu Sufyan remarked, 'Never have I seen anyone loving someone with such devotion as Muhammad's followers love him.'"

Similar to this is the story of 'Abdullah ibn Zayd, may Allah be pleased with him. When his son brought the news of the Prophet's death, he cried in earnest prayer to Allah, "O Lord! Blind my eyes, so that I may never see anyone after my beloved Muhammad!" Allah answered his prayer and he became blind."[1]

To love the Messenger, may Allah bless him and grant him peace, leads to obeying him and thus following the right path of the *Shari'a* and the *Sunna* at all times. Anyone who loves the Prophet will follow precisely in the footsteps of the one he loves. Allah Most High says: *"You have indeed in the Messenger of Allah a beautiful pattern (of conduct) for any whose hope is Allah and the Final Day, and who engages much in the remembrance of Allah"* (33:21). The noble Prophet himself said: "Whoever loves a people will be with them in the Hereafter."[2] Likewise, it is imperative that we follow the *Sunna* of the Prophet, may Allah bless him and grant him peace. He said: "Follow my *Sunna* and that of the rightly-guided Caliphs after me, and hold to it firmly."[3]

The *Sunna* of Allah's Messenger is next to the Glorious Qur'an in importance. It explains the Qur'an, clarifying its rules and injunctions as well as their objectives. Some of the verses in the Qur'an were revealed as general or specific provisions and it is the *hadiths* of the Prophet which explain and define the divine purpose in each verse. In this respect, Allah Most High says: *"We have sent down upon you the Reminder that you may explain to mankind that which has been sent to them."* (16:44) For instance, Allah has given general commands to observe the prayer and the *zakat*, and to carry out certain punishments against adulterers, thieves and wine-drinkers, but it is the *Sunna* of the Messenger that elucidates the meaning of prayer and *zakat* and the times and

---

1. Az-Zurqani, *al-Mawahib al-laduniyya*, vol. i, 292.
2. Narrated by al-Hakim in *al-Mustadrak*.
3. Narrated by Abu Dawud and at-Tirmidhi.

manner in which they are to be performed and specifies the conditions within which the legal punishments are to be implemented. Allah Almighty orders us to obey the Messenger, may Allah bless him and grant him peace, to implement his commands, and never to disobey him in the following verse: *"So take what the Messenger assigns to you and deny yourselves that which he withholds from you"* (59:7). He says in another verse: *"It is not fitting for a believer, man or woman, when Allah and His Messenger have decreed a certain matter, to have any choice"* (33:36).

It is true that the Prophet, may Allah bless him and grant him peace, was a human being, but he was different in that he received Revelation. Allah moulded him in His sight, protected him with love, kindness and mercy, made him the epitome of high morals and fine character. A man stood before Allah's Messenger on the day Makka was conquered. But out of awe and high respect, he remained in his place, unable to move. The Prophet said to him, "Relax, for I am no more than a man whose mother used to eat dried meat in Makka."

The Prophet, may Allah bless him and grant him peace, on several occasions showed mercy and kindness even to the tyrants and transgressors of Quraysh. He treated with kindness the people who had persecuted and fought him at Makka, plotted to kill him, and tormented his Companions. Everyone in Makka expected him to take revenge on them when he conquered the city, yet he did nothing of the sort. He turned to them after he had finished his speech and said, "What do you expect me to do with you?" They said, "Nothing but goodness." He said, "Go, you are free."

Most of them converted to Islam immediately while some others held back in hesitation, including Safwan ibn Umayya and 'Ikrima ibn Abi Jahl, who attempted to fight at al-Khandama. The Prophet, may Allah bless him and grant him peace, sent Khalid ibn al-Walid, who defeated them. They tried to escape, but the wife of 'Ikrima, who was a Muslim, asked Allah's Messenger, may Allah bless him and grant him peace, to grant him immunity, and he did so. When Safwan travelled to Jeddah, 'Umayr ibn Wahb said to the Messenger of Allah, "Safwan ibn Umayya, who is master of his people, fled to throw himself into the sea." The Messenger of

Allah, may Allah bless him and grant him peace, said, "He has been granted immunity." 'Umayr said, "Give me a sign which will assure him." The Prophet gave him his turban which he was wearing the day he entered Makka. 'Umayr went to Jeddah and found Safwan just before he set sail. He brought him back to Makka with the Prophet's turban as a sign of immunity and so no Muslim stood in their way. Safwan asked the Messenger for two month's respite to make up his mind, but he was given four. Before they expired he accepted Islam.

The Prophet instructed his Companions who had been calling 'Ikrima "Ibn Abi Jahl" not to give him this name, not to hurt his feelings or stain his honour by recalling the disgraceful deeds of his father and his disbelief. (Ibn Abi Jahl literally means 'the son of the Father of Ignorance'.) Such was the Messenger of Allah in his noble character, modesty, gentleness and forbearance, and love for his community. He thus won the hearts which loved him and the religion he brought. His most bitter enemies came to serve him, and were ready to sacrifice their lives, children, and wealth for the sake of Islam.

Teach your children all of this. Sit with them at different times and tell them about the noble life of the Prophet, may Allah bless him and grant him peace. It is an occasion for us to renew our awareness of those great and momentous events, the memory of which has survived for more than fourteen hundred years. They live forever as a light and guidance for humanity.

We pray to Allah to deepen our faith in Him and love for His Prophet.

Chapter Two
He was Born an Orphan

The Messenger, may Allah bless him and grant him peace, becoming an orphan was a mercy, just as his poverty was a blessing. Allah Himself took care of his education and upbringing. "My Lord educated me, and He gave me the best education."

The Messenger, may Allah bless him and grant him peace, was born an orphan. His father had gone to Syria with one of the caravans of Quraysh. On his return, he stopped at Yathrib to buy provisions as his father 'Abdu'l-Muttalib had told him to. But he fell ill and died. He was buried there.

Allah's Messenger, may Allah bless him and grant him peace, was fated to come into this world as an orphan. But Allah protected him from the bitter feeling of orphanhood at this early stage by entrusting him to the tender love and care of his grandfather, 'Abdu'l-Muttalib. Allah also gave him three kind and loving mothers: his natural mother, Amina, who was pure and tender; his nursing mother, Halima as-Sa'diyya; and his mother who adopted him and brought him up, Umm Ayman Baraka from Abyssinia.

In the sixth year of his life, his mother and her servant Baraka went with him to Yathrib to visit the grave of his father and introduce him to his relatives from the Najjar tribe. They remained in Yathrib for a while, and then prepared for the return journey. On the way, Amina suddenly felt a great pain, which increased along the way. She looked at her son and cried with a voice weakened by agony: "Every living thing must die. Everything new must grow old. Everything great must pass away. I am dying, but my memory shall remain, for I bequeath a good omen, and have given birth to a pure son."

She then surrendered her spirit to her Creator, leaving her son with Baraka, his nurse. Baraka took him and he returned to his grandfather broken-hearted, fatherless and motherless. His grandfather took care of him and showed him more kindness than before, compensating him for his mother's care and love.

According to Ibn Ishaq: "A rug used to be spread out for 'Abdu'l-Muttalib beside the Ka'ba. His children would sit awaiting his arrival but none of them would sit on it out of respect for him. Muhammad, however, would come and sit upon it and his uncles would take him and seat him away from it. 'Abdu'l-Muttalib used to say whenever he saw them doing this, "Leave my son, for I swear by Allah that a great destiny awaits him." He would then seat him on the rug and gently pass his hand over him, pleased with the things that he saw him doing."

When Muhammad was eight years of age, his grandfather fell very ill and felt that death was near. He confided the boy to the care of his son, Abu Talib. Abu Talib spared no effort to look after him after 'Abdu'l-Muttalib died. He took Muhammad with him wherever he went, so that he would not feel isolated or deprived. Fatima bint Asad, Abu Talib's wife, was kind to him as well. She favoured him over his own children when she saw the nobility of his character and the blessedness of his nature.

The presence of Muhammad, may Allah bless him and grant him peace, in the house of Abu Talib brought blessings as it did in the house of Halima as-Sa'diyya and provisions were abundant. It is well known that Abu Talib lived in difficult circumstances and had many dependants to support. When his children ate alone they seemed never to be satisfied but when they ate in the company of Muhammad there was always food left over. Abu Talib used to say to him, "Truly, you are kind to your kinsfolk."[1]

The Blessed Orphan

Muhammad ibn 'Abdullah was a mercy and blessing to his people and to all mankind even when he was still in his mother's

---

1 Ibn Hisham, citing Ibn Ishaq, *as-Sirat an-Nabawiyya*, i, 176.

womb. For it was at that time that Almighty Allah defeated Abraha and his army, who tried to conquer Makka and destroy the noble Ka'ba. On that victorious day, Muhammad was born. When he became a Messenger, the Holy Ka'ba became even more sacred, more revered, and once again a destination for many nations.

We should not forget the blessings which he brought to Halima as-Sa'diyya. She had come from her desert homeland with other nurses to find children to nurse during a year of drought. The orphan was shown to them all but none of them accepted him except Halima.

Halima said: "We went out to Makka on a skinny donkey, with an aged camel which did not give even a drop of milk. We could not sleep at night because our child was crying out of hunger. But when I put Muhammad on my lap, my breasts overflowed with milk. He drank until he was quenched, and so did my son, and they both slept. My husband went to his camel and milked her. We drank to our satisfaction, sleeping peacefully that night. In the morning, I rode the donkey carrying Muhammad with me. We moved faster than all other nurses. My companions said, 'Daughter of Abu Dhu'ayb! Slow down! Is that the donkey on which you came?' Yes,' I told them, 'It is the same.' They said, 'By Allah, this is something remarkable.' We came to the deserts of the Sa'd tribe. No other lands are more barren than ours but we found them green and alive. My sheep grazed to their full and we drank milk, although no one else could. People said to their shepherds, 'Follow the tracks of the daughter of Abu Dhu'ayb.' My husband said, 'O Halima! You brought us a blessed baby.'"

After having completed breast-feeding, Muhammad was returned to Makka where he led a blessed life. Then Allah sent the message of Islam to him and thus the blessing proved universal, as mankind was saved from the darkness of ignorance and guided to the light of truth, justice, and peace.

According to Imam Abu Zahra[1], "Compassion is nurtured by the pain and sufferings which individuals undergo in life. No one is more merciful than someone who has tasted the bitterness of

1. Muhammad Abu Zahra, *Khatam an-Nabiyyin*, i, 130-1.

weakness, and what weakness could be more severe than orphan-hood?

Certainly, there can be no doubt that the intimate relationship between Muhammad the orphan and the Abyssinian servant-woman Umm Ayman was a divine gift which filled his heart with the conviction that all people were equal and that the best of them were the best in deed. It is not their lineage of which they should be proud. It was certainly Allah's wisdom that decided Muhammad's indispensable nurse to be an Abyssinian servant-woman. Had he been brought up by a woman from one of the ruling families, it would have been said that the noble character which he attained was solely the work of his nurse. Since he was brought up by an Abyssinian servant-woman, however, no such claim could have been made; his educator was Allah alone.

The Messenger of Allah, may Allah bless him and grant him peace, spoke, as always, the truth when he said, "My Lord has educated me and given me the best education." Allah Himself says: *"Truly, yours is a tremendous character."* His was a character which offered a real challenge to all humanity for each and everyone to improve. Allah says: *"Did He not find you an orphan, and give you refuge? Did He not find you astray, and guide you? Did He not find you needy, and give you satisfaction? ... And as for the blessing of your Lord, proclaim it!"* (93:6-11)

The Prophet said, "I am the best of Adam's descendants, and this is no boast." For he is the best in upbringing, behaviour, guidance and status in the sight of Allah, who educated him and gave him the best education. He is thus the ideal model for all mankind.

In the light of this, it is not surprising that he once grew extremely angry when he heard one of his Companions insulting another with the words: "Son of a black woman!" The Prophet said, "That is enough! That is enough! That is enough! The son of a white woman is not better than the son of a black woman unless it be by piety and righteousness."

Muhammad was the son of a white woman and was nursed by a black woman, thus becoming a son to both. It is well known that Allah's Messenger, may Allah bless him and grant him peace, used to say about Umm Ayman: "She was my mother after my mother."

He was very kind to her and did everything to please her and bring her joy.

From Poverty to Wealth

When the Prophet's father, 'Abdullah, died, he left for his family the servant-woman (Baraka), five camels, and a few sheep. This inheritance reduced Muhammad to the rank of the poor. So he had to work to earn his living and as a boy he occupied himself with herding sheep for which he earned a few coins. With some of this money he used to buy food for the family of Abu Talib, while he gave the rest to the poor.

Without question, his work as a shepherd was part of the Divine Plan. All Prophets before him had been shepherds, an occupation which teaches gentleness towards the weak, patience, and leadership. Ibn Ishaq relates that Allah's Messenger, may Allah bless him and grant him peace, said, "Every Prophet worked as a shepherd." "Even you, O Messenger of Allah?" he was asked. "Even me," he replied.[1] In *ar-Rawd al-Anuf*, the author explains that "Allah the Exalted made Prophets start as shepherds so that they could lead their people."[2]

When he grew older, the Prophet, may Allah bless him and grant him peace, busied himself with commerce, travelling with his uncle to Syria. He grew up protected and safeguarded by Allah, who wished to prepare him for His Message and save him from the corrupt practices of Quraysh.

Allah then granted him something of His wealth. He took care of the business caravans of Khadija, the richest and most noble woman of her age. He returned with profits which were many times greater than those of other merchants. She trusted his honesty and management of commercial affairs. She married him and put her entire wealth at his disposal. His honesty, wisdom and good management brought him vast wealth. She gave him her love, loyalty, and wealth.

1. Ibn Hisham, *as-Sira*, 1, 174.
2. *Ar-Rawd al-Anuf*, i, 11 (Moroccan edition).

The Great are Those whom Allah Makes Great

Ja'far as-Sadiq, may Allah be pleased with him, said, "The Messenger of Allah, may Allah bless him and grant him peace, was born an orphan so that he would have no duties towards anyone."[1]

Ibn 'Ammar writes in *Kashf al-Huda*, "Allah made him an orphan because everyone great starts modestly. The Prophet, at the height of his glory, would look at his beginnings and know that greatness is from Allah and that his strength did not come from his parents or his wealth, but from Allah alone. The matter was thus decreed so that he might feel compassion for the poor and the orphan."

> His orphanhood was a blessing and a mercy;
> His poverty was a gift and kindness;
> His Lord brought him up, and honoured him;
> He educated him, and gave him the best education.

We read in the Qur'an:

"A Messenger has come to you from among yourselves, grievous to him is your suffering, who is solicitous for you; gentle and merciful towards the believers." (10:128)

"We sent you only as a mercy to the worlds!" (21:107)

"Who allowed for them what is good and wholesome, and forbade uncleanness to them, relieving them of the burden and the shackles which had been upon them, and guided them, by the leave of their Lord, to the Straight Path." (7:157)

"O you who believe! Bless him and greet him most abundantly!" (33:56)

---

1. *Subul al-Huda*, i, 393.

Chapter Three
Celebrating the Noble Mawlud (Birth) of the Prophet

During the blessed month of Rabi' al-Awwal, with the moon almost full, on the night of the twelfth, millions of Muslims in every corner of the earth are happy to celebrate the birth of the Prophet, may Allah bless him and grant him peace. They read the life story of the man who brought guidance and happiness. They learn about his morals and attributes, for he was the Unlettered Prophet who had all the noble and perfect characteristics and the highest ideals. Allah Almighty said to him: *"Truly yours is a tremendous character."* (68:4)

Without doubt, the best way to celebrate this occasion is to read his *Sira* and explain it to the young. This will induce them to love the Messenger of Allah more and study his way of life, that of his noble family, his rightly guided Successors and his Companions, may Allah be pleased with all of them.

It is most desirable and highly recommended to sit together for that noble purpose in a true Islamic atmosphere without unacceptable innovations or deviations. Although the Messenger, may Allah bless him and grant him peace, should be mentioned and remembered at every moment, nevertheless, in the month of Rabi' al-Awwal, people's attachment to him grows since it is the month of his birth. However, scholars do not state that the celebration of the *Mawlud* on any particular night is a *sunna*. In fact, they consider that such an attitude would be an innovation since it was not practised by the Companions of Allah's Messenger, may Allah bless him and grant him peace, whose love and remembrance of him was perpetual: *"Truly, Allah and his Angels send blessings on the Prophet. O you who believe! Send blessings on him and salute him with all respect."* (22:56)

Secondly, it should be remembered that the Prophet, may Allah bless him and grant him peace, himself used to celebrate the day of his birth and show gratitude to Allah for His great blessings upon him. He used to fast on this day as stated in the *hadith* related by Abu Qatada. The Messenger of Allah, may Allah bless him and grant him peace, was once asked about fasting on Mondays. He replied, "On that day I was born, and on that day I received the Revelation."[1]

This establishes the principle of celebrating his *Mawlud,* although its forms may differ. Nonetheless the essence is there, whether marked by fasting, feeding the poor, or gathering to remember him, invoking blessings upon him, or studying his perfect attributes.

Thirdly, to feel happiness when remembering the Prophet, may Allah bless him and grant him peace, is required by a command of the Qur'an: *"Say, by the grace of Allah and His mercy; let them rejoice in that"* (10:58). The Muslims should rejoice when recalling the Prophet of Allah, of whom Allah says: *"We have sent you only as a mercy to the worlds"* (21:107).

Fourthly, the Prophet, may Allah bless him and grant him peace, was fully aware of the significant relation between time and major religious events of the past. Such occasions provide an opportunity to commemorate them and celebrate the day on which they occurred. This principle was established by the Prophet, may Allah bless him and grant him peace, himself. Thus when he arrived in Madina, he found the Jews fasting the day of 'Ashura' in commemoration of the day on which Allah rescued their Prophet Moses and drowned their enemy. So they fasted in thanksgiving to Allah. The Prophet, may Allah bless him and grant him peace, said, "We are more worthy of Moses than you are." So he fasted on that day and instructed the Muslims to do the same.

---

1. Related by Imam Muslim in the Book of Fasting in his *Sahih.*

Chapter Four
Muhammad as a Father

Baraka (Umm Ayman) was hurrying through the marketplace, her face shining with joy. She met Sulayma al-Khuza'iyya, who said to her in amazement: "What has happened, Baraka? Why are you running so fast?"

"I have good news for the Prophet."

"What good news?"

"Khadija has given birth to her fourth daughter!"

Sulayma looked closely at her and asked her in astonishment: "Is a fourth daughter good news?"

"Of course!"

Sulayma drew close to her and whispered, "Speak the truth, Baraka."

"About what?"

"How is your master going to receive the news of another girl?"

Baraka laughed and said, "Your question reminds me of the day when Khadija gave birth to her first daughter, Zaynab. I was told to convey the news to the Prophet. So I went to him, trembling with fear, afraid that he would bury me alive with the baby. But an amazing surprise was in store for me."

"How?"

"As soon as he heard that his wife had given birth to a girl, his face brightened with light and joy. He rushed to see the baby, joyfully carried her in his arms, kissing her and congratulating her mother. He then ordered that some animals be slaughtered and a feast held to celebrate her birth."

Baraka set off and Sulayma remained deep in thought. She had experienced the bitterness of losing three children whom her husband had buried alive, paying no heed to her tears and imploring supplications. This was a common practice at the time. Whoever did not bury his infant daughter would treat her with disgust and debasement. He would say to her on her way to her groom's house, "I hope you will have sons, not daughters. May Allah bring forth from you glory, plenitude and strength." This he would say if the groom was a relative. If he was not, it was customary to say, "May you not be blessed with sons, for you will bring the aliens closer, and you will give birth to a stranger."[1]

Sulayma appreciated the Prophet's action as something truly remarkable and wished that all fathers, especially her husband, would follow his example. At that time, she did not know that Muhammad was the "mercy bestowed to the world"; that he would be sent as a Messenger with the True Religion which prohibited the burying of girls alive and honoured women, asserting that males and females spring from one soul: *"O mankind! Fear your Lord, who created you from one soul, and created its spouse therefrom, and spread from them a multitude of men and women"* (4:1). Allah revealed a complete and perfect Law which gave women their appropriate positions in society and assured them a noble and dignified life as daughters, sisters, wives and mothers.

The attitude of Allah's Messenger to the birth of daughters was that of a human father receiving them with joy and happiness. He thus set the example to those whose hearts had grown hard, cruel and devoid of mercy. Allah says: *"And when one of them is given the good news of a daughter, his face darkens, he is filled with rage; he hides from people because of the bad news he has been given, (asking himself): shall he keep it in contempt, or bury it beneath the dust? Evil is their judgement"* (16:59). How could Allah's Messenger have been other than he was, when Allah Himself had told him: *"We have sent you but as a mercy to the worlds"* (21:107)?

---

1. Ibn Habib, *al-Muhabbar*, 310.

26

His Children by his First Wife

The Messenger of Allah, may Allah bless him and grant him peace, had four daughters by his first wife, Khadija bint Khuwaylid, Mother of the Believers: Zaynab, Ruqayya, Umm Kulthum, and Fatima az-Zahra. These flowers grew and blossomed in an atmosphere of affection, purity, honour and dignity under the guardianship, love and compassion of the Messenger of Allah and the experienced care of Khadija.

Zaynab married Abu al-'As ibn ar-Rabi', the son of her maternal aunt. Ruqayya and Umm Kulthum married 'Utba and 'Utayba, the two sons of Abu Lahab, the Prophet's uncle. Fatima remained at home, being too young for marriage. When the Messenger of Allah, may Allah bless him and grant him peace, received his message and Khadija embraced Islam, the four followed her. The Messenger of Allah started implementing the commands of Allah and calling people to Islam. Quraysh refused to accept his call and made every effort to obstruct and plot against him.

One day, the great men of Quraysh gathered together to decide how to get rid of him. One of them said, "You are bearing his own troubles on his behalf! Abu'l-'As has married Zaynab while Ruqayya and Umm Kulthum have married 'Utba and 'Utayba. Let them be divorced, therefore, and he will be busy with them and have no time for the new religion he is trying to impose on us."

The three husbands were hesitant, however, for each of them loved his wife and would not be able to do without her or find a better wife. But Umm Jamil, the malicious unbeliever, was determined to carry out the decision of Quraysh. She said to her two sons, "I disclaim you as my sons if you don't divorce the daughters of Muhammad and return them to his house!"

Both sons obeyed their mother's instructions, so Ruqayya and Umm Kulthum returned to their father's home. They did not stay there long, however, for Ruqayya soon married 'Uthman ibn 'Affan, a great hero, one of the first eight to accept Islam and one of the ten people promised Heaven by the Prophet, may Allah bless him and grant him peace. He emigrated with her first to

Abyssinia. Then they travelled to Madina where she fell sick and died on the day the victory of Badr was announced.

'Uthman, may Allah be pleased with him, grieved much for her, and her losing his blessed position as the Prophet's son-in-law. Prophet's Messenger, may Allah bless him and grant him peace, saw his grief and asked him about it. He replied, "Has any man experienced my affliction, Messenger of Allah? The daughter of Allah's Messenger has died, and the kinship which was between us has come to an end."

The Prophet, may Allah bless him and grant him peace, consoled him and gave him Umm Kulthum, her sister, in marriage. She remained with him until she passed away after six years of marriage, in the ninth year of the Hijra."[1] It is said that he was called Dhu'l-Nurayn, "Man of the Two Lights", because he married both Ruqayya and Umm Kulthum, the daughters of the Prophet, may Allah bless him and grant him peace. No one but 'Uthman was so honoured. Others said that he was called that because the Prophet, may Allah bless him and grant him peace, said of him, "In heaven, he is called Dhu'n-Nurayn". It is well-known that he used to read the entire Qur'an every night during his prayers, and both the Qur'an and prayers at night are sources of light.

As for Abu'l-'As, Quraysh told him, "Divorce your wife, and we shall give you any Qurayshite woman you wish." But he replied, "No, by Allah, I shall never leave my wife and shall never accept any other woman of Quraysh as a substitute."[2]

Tragic events then followed. Abu Talib's death was followed by Khadija's a few days later. The Messenger, may Allah bless him and grant him peace, made his *hijra*, and settled in Madina with his Companions.

They fought the battle of Badr and many of the leaders of Quraysh were killed, while others, including Abu'l-'As, were captured. His family were ready to pay the ransom which amounted to four thousand dirhams, but Zaynab decided that he should be ransomed with something more precious than money. She sent her

1. Al-'Aqqad, *Dhu'n-Nurayn 'Uthman ibn 'Affan*, 78-9.
2. Ibn Hisham, *as-Sira*, ii, 219.

father the necklace that her mother had given her as a wedding present when she married Abu'l-'As.

According to Ibn Ishaq, "When Allah's Messenger, may Allah bless him and grant him peace, saw the necklace, he felt deeply sorry for her and said, "If you wish, you may free her captive and give her back her money."

"Yes, Messenger of Allah," they said. So they restored it to her. The Messenger of Allah, may Allah bless him and grant him peace, asked Abu'l-'As to release Zaynab and he promised to do so. When Abu'l-'As arrived in Makka, he ordered his brother Kinana to take her. So they left. On their way, Habbar ibn al-Aswad and another man attacked them. Habbar threatened her with his lance. She fell down and, as she was pregnant, she suffered a miscarriage. Kinana shouted in rage, "By Allah, if any one of you comes near me I will shoot him with my arrows." So, the men drew back.

Abu Sufyan came and rebuked Kinana for having gone out with her during daylight. He ordered him to return and wait until the people calmed down and then leave with her by night.

When Allah's Messenger, may Allah bless him and grant him peace, learnt about this incident, he became angry and ordered that Habbar and his companion be burnt. The following day he said, "I had commanded you earlier to burn those two men if you capture them but I remembered that only Allah can punish by fire. So if you capture them, kill them."[1]

After this, Abu'l-'As went to Zaynab seeking her protection. His caravan was captured by a Muslim military unit including Zayd ibn al-Haritha with a hundred and seventy men on his return from Syria to Makka. Zaynab went out to the mosque where the Messenger of Allah, may Allah bless him and grant him peace, was about to begin the prayer and called out, "O people! I have given my protection to Abu'l-'As ibn ar-Rabi'!" When the Prophet, may Allah bless him and grant him peace, finished his prayer, he asked, "Did you hear what I heard?" "Yes," they replied. He said, "I swear by Allah, I knew nothing of this matter until now. The most modest of the Muslims is able to give protection."

---

1. Ibn Ishaq, *as-Sira*, ii, 223.

He left the mosque and went to see his daughter. He said to her, "My daughter, be hospitable to him, but let him not approach you, for he is unlawful to you."[1]

The Muslims returned to Abu'l-'As his trading goods, so he went back to Makka. There he delivered the goods to their owners and declared, "I bear witness that there is no deity save Allah and that Muhammad is the Messenger of Allah. By Allah, I did not want to convert to Islam before now lest you should suspect my integrity, for I wanted to return your goods to you. Now that Allah helped me to deliver the trust, I declare my Islam."

Then he left Makka to Madina where he met Allah's Messenger, who praised him and gave him Zaynab back. A year later, she died, leaving Umama and 'Ali. It is said that Umama looked like her mother, and the Prophet found in her much solace for the loss of his daughter. He loved her a great deal and showed her tremendous compassion. It is narrated by al-Bukhari and Muslim that the Prophet, may Allah bless him and grant him peace, used to carry her on his shoulder and pray and, whenever he prostrated, he put her down and then he would carry her again.

The fourth daughter of the Prophet was Fatima az-Zahra about whom 'A'isha, may Allah be pleased with her, said, "I never saw anyone better than Fatima, except her father."

The Messenger of Allah, may Allah bless him and grant him peace, said, "Fatima is the noblest of the ladies of Paradise."[2] He also said about her, "Fatima is part of me. Whoever angers her, angers me."[3] 'A'isha is reported to have said, "Whenever Fatima came in, the Prophet stood up for her, kissed her, and gave her his seat. Whenever the Prophet came in, she stood up for him, kissed him, and gave her her seat.'"[4]

'A'isha, may Allah be pleased with her, said, "Fatima once came walking in the same manner as the Prophet, may Allah bless him and grant him peace. He welcomed her and seated her on his right-hand side. Then he whispered something in her ear and she wept. He spoke to her again, and she smiled. I asked her what he

1. Ibn Ishaq, *as-Sira*, ii, 234.
2. Narrated by al-Bukhari.
3. Narrated by al-Bukhari.
4. Narrated by at-Tirmidhi, Abu Dawud and an-Nasa'i.

had said. She replied, 'I wouldn't reveal the secret of Allah's Messenger.' But when he died, I asked her again and she said, 'He told me, "Gabriel used to go over the Qur'an with me once every year, but this year he did so twice. I can only surmise that my life has run its course. You shall be the first of my family to join me." At this I wept, but he then said, "Are you not happy that you will be the noblest of the ladies of Paradise?" When I heard this, I smiled.'"

When Allah revealed the following verse, *"And admonish your nearest kin"* (26:214), Allah's Messenger called his people, "O family of 'Abd Manaf! I cannot protect you from Allah's decree! O 'Abbas ibn 'Abdu'l-Muttalib! I cannot protect you from Allah's decree! O Safiyya bint 'Abdu'l-Muttalib! I cannot protect you from Allah's decree! O Fatima bint Muhammad! I cannot protect you from Allah's decree!"

Fatima witnessed the tyranny and brutality of Quraysh against her father when she was still a little girl. They used to oppress him, making fun of his religion. She saw one of them grab his cloak trying to strangle him while Abu Bakr protected him from their tyranny. He said to them, "Would you kill a man who says, 'My God is Allah'?" Fatima saw and heard this. She wept and felt sad about the hardship her father was experiencing.

On another occasion, she was at the Ka'ba when 'Uqba ibn Mu'ayt threw the intestines of a camel over the back of the Messenger, may Allah bless him and grant him peace, while he was praying. She ran over to her father and removed the filth from him and prayed against 'Uqba. The Messenger of Allah, may Allah bless him and grant him peace, raised his head and prayed to Allah to punish the leaders of Quraysh: Abu Jahl, 'Utba, Shayba, 'Uqba ibn Abi Mu'ayt, al-Walid ibn 'Utba, and Umayya ibn Khalaf.

When Fatima was eighteen years old, Abu Bakr, may Allah be pleased with him, asked to marry her. The Prophet, may Allah bless him and grant him peace, told him, "Abu Bakr! Wait for Allah's decree!"

Then 'Umar, may Allah be pleased with him, came and asked for her hand in marriage and he gave him the same answer. 'Ali

31

came, his shyness visible on his face, to propose to her, and the following event took place, as he later described it:

"When I sat down in front of him, I remained speechless, unable to say a word.

'What brings you here?' the Prophet inquired. 'Do you want something?' I remained silent.

He said, 'Perhaps you have come to ask for Fatima's hand?'

'Yes,' I said."

So the Messenger of Allah, may Allah bless him and grant him peace, married them to one another. When she heard the news, she wept. The Prophet asked her, "Why are you weeping, Fatima? By Allah, I have given you in marriage to the most gentle, the most learned of them, and the first to embrace Islam."

On the night when 'Ali and Fatima were married, the Messenger of Allah, may Allah bless him and grant him peace, called for some water with which he made his ablution, and then sprinkled it over her, saying, "O Allah! Bless them and bless their progeny."

'Ali, may Allah be pleased with him, asked the Prophet, may Allah bless him and grant him peace, "Whom do you love more, Fatima or me?" He replied, "She is more beloved to me than you are and you are dearer to me than she is."

The Messenger's love and affection for Fatima and his compassionate fatherhood were obvious when he learnt that 'Ali had intended to marry a woman from Makhzum, the daughter of 'Amr ibn Hisham (Abu Jahl), the enemy of Allah and His Messenger.

The Prophet, may Allah bless him and grant him peace, went to the mosque and stood in anger on the pulpit and said to his Companions, "The family of Hisham ibn al-Mughira have asked permission to give their daughter in marriage to 'Ali ibn Abi Talib. I do not give permission! I do not give permission! I do not give permission! Unless the son of Abu Talib chooses to divorce my daughter and marry their daughter. For my daughter is part of me. What hurts her feelings hurts my feelings. I am afraid that her faith may be affected."

He then mentioned Abu'l-'As ibn ar-Rabi' and highly praised him as a husband and son-in-law. Then he said, "He spoke to me and was truthful. He promised me and fulfilled his promise. I forbid nothing which is lawful nor do I permit anything which is forbidden but Allah will never unite the daughter of Allah's Messenger and the daughter of His enemy in one house."[1]

At-Tirmidhi reported that 'A'isha, may Allah be pleased with her, was asked, "Who is the most beloved to the Prophet, may Allah bless him and grant him peace?" She said, "Fatima." They asked, "And among men?" She said, "Her husband, who was to my knowledge always fasting and praying."

Fatima az-Zahra gave birth to al-Hasan, al-Husayn, Zaynab and Umm Kulthum, all of whom the Messenger loved dearly. Regarding al-Hasan and al-Husayn he said, "O Allah! I love them, so love them and love those who love them."[2]

In another narration, he said, "O Allah, love those who love them and abhor those who hate them."[3]

It is reported that Allah's Messenger was once accompanied by 'Ali, holding al-Hasan by one hand and al-Husayn by the other. When they entered, he seated 'Ali and Fatima near to him and put al-Hasan and al-Husayn on his lap. He then covered them with his cloak and read the following verse, *"And Allah only wishes to remove all abomination from you, members of the House, and to make you pure and spotless"* (33:33). Then he said, "O Allah! These are the people of my House. Make them pure."[4]

On another occasion, the Prophet's fatherly affection was manifest for all to see. He was seen carrying one of his grandsons to the mosque on his shoulder. When he arrived, and the prayer began, he put him gently to one side and led the people in prayer. Those present in the mosque were surprised by the length the Prophet remained in prostration. When the prayer was finished, they asked him, "Messenger of Allah! You prostrated for so long that we thought that something had happened or that you had received some Revelation!" But he replied, "It was not that. My grandson

---

1. Al-Bukhari, *Sahih*, xxix, 538; Muslim, *Sahih*, xiv, 44; Abu Dawud, *Sunan*, xii; at-Tirmidhi, *Sunan*, xlvi; Ibn Maja, *Sunan*, ix, 56; Ibn Hanbal, *Musnad*, iv, 326-9.
2. Narrated by at-Tirmidhi in *al-Manaqib*.
3. Narrated by at-Tabarani in *al-Kabir* and by Ibn Abi Shayba.
4. Narrated by at-Tirmidhi.

climbed onto my back and I was reluctant to disturb him before he was finished."[1]

People used to see him holding al-Husayn by his shoulders while the latter was putting his feet on the Prophet's chest. The Prophet would tell him, "Open your mouth." Then he kissed him, saying, "O Allah! I love him, so love him and love those who love him!"[2]

Someone, being astonished at the way the Prophet, may Allah bless him and grant him peace, kissed his grandson, once said, "Look at the way he kisses his grandson! By Allah, I have children and I have never kissed any of them!" Allah's Messenger, may Allah bless him and grant him peace, said, "He who feels no compassion receives no compassion."

In the last days of his life, while he was in great pain, Fatima saw him overwhelmed by agony. She said, "My father is in great agony." He replied, "There shall be no more agony for your father after this day." When he died, she said, "Father! Rest in peace in Paradise." When he was buried, she said to the people in the procession, "Was it easy for you to put earth over the Prophet, may Allah bless him and grant him peace?"

Allah's Messenger also had a son by Khadija named al-Qasim; hence his famous nickname, 'Abu'l-Qasim'. He also had 'Abdullah, who was named the "Pure and Good One" as he was born after the advent of prophethood.[3] Both these sons died in infancy: although it is said that al-Qasim grew old enough to walk, yet he had not completed his breast-feeding period when he died. Imam as-Suhayli writes in his book, *ar-Rawd al-Anuf*, that Allah's Messenger once came into the house of Khadija after he had received his Message. He found her crying, "O Messenger of Allah!" she said, "my milk still flows for al-Qasim! If only he had lived to finish his breast-feeding." He told her, "He will complete his breast-feeding in Paradise."

---

1. Narrated by an-Nasa'i and by Imam Ahmad in his *Musnad*.
2. Muslim, *Sahih, Fada'il*, iv, 1882.
3. As-Suhayli, *ar-Rawd al-Anuf*, i, 123; Ibn Hajar, *al-Isaba*, vii, 61; *as-Sira*, i, 202.

Ibrahim, "the Eye's Delight"

The Prophet, may Allah bless him and grant him peace, had a son Ibrahim by his Coptic wife, Maria. The child resembled his father a great deal and the resemblance increased as he grew older. The Messenger of Allah, may Allah bless him and grant him peace, was deeply attached to him, perhaps because he was born after the deaths of al-Qasim, 'Abdullah, Zaynab, Ruqayya, Umm Kulthum, and Khadija herself. And yet the Prophet's happiness with Ibrahim did not last, for Ibrahim became very sick. When he was dying, the Prophet, may Allah bless him and grant him peace, was informed. He leaned on the arm of 'Abdu'r-Rahman ibn 'Awf, deeply grieving. They went to the place where Ibrahim was lying. Ibrahim was dying in his mother's lap. He laid him on his own lap, his heart heavy with sorrow, and his grief clearly visible on his face. He said, "Ibrahim, I cannot protect you from the will of Allah." Tears welled up in his eyes as the little boy breathed his last. Maria and his sister were crying but the Prophet, may Allah bless him and grant him peace, did not stop them.[1]

With Ibrahim a lifeless body, tears filled the Prophet's eyes and he said, "O Ibrahim! If it were not that death is Allah's decree and promise and that we all die and the last shall follow the first, we would grieve for you even more." Then he was silent for a while, and added, "The eye weeps, the heart grieves, and we say only what pleases the Lord. Ibrahim, we are indeed sad for you."

Once the Prophet, may Allah bless him and grant him peace, paid a visit to Sa'd ibn 'Ubada who was sick. He found him surrounded by his family. The Prophet cried for him. When everybody saw him crying, they cried as well. The Prophet said, "Listen, Allah does not punish those who shed tears or feel sadness in heart. He punishes or forgives for this," and he pointed to his tongue.

Ibrahim's death coincided with a solar eclipse, which the Muslims considered a miracle. "The sun has eclipsed because he has died!" they said. The Prophet, may Allah bless him and grant him peace, was annoyed at this, and spoke to them, saying, "The

---

1. Muhammad Husayn Haykal, *Hayat Muhammad*, p. 464.

sun and the moon are two signs of Allah. They do not eclipse for the death or birth of anyone. When you see an eclipse, remember Allah and offer prayer to Him."

This event shows clearly the greatness of Allah's Messenger. Although he was overcome with grief and sadness, he did not forget his Message or fail to speak the truth. Instead, he addressed his people to correct their misunderstanding.

Certainly, the Messenger of Allah, may Allah bless him and grant him peace, had a passionate love for his children but his love for his message was greater still!

Chapter Five
The Noble Hijra

The Emigration, *al-Hijra*, was a victory granted by Allah and a triumph for the believers. It marked the beginning of the history of Islam. The descent of the Glorious Qur'an upon the Seal of the Messengers and Prophets, Muhammad ibn 'Abdullah, may Allah bless him and grant him peace, was the most important event in the history of Islam. Without question, the *Hijra* was the second most important. It represented the victory of Islam, whereby the Muslims became firmly established and the foundation of the first Islamic state was laid. Religion had now moved from the theoretical to the practical phase, creating a society which implemented its rulings in its spirit, its system, its legislation, its practices and its conduct.

The *Hijra* was the starting point for many other victories, including the battles at Badr, Makka, Hunayn and elsewhere. The *Hijra* provided the Muslims with a definite point from which to determine their history. Prior to Islam, the Arabs used to specify dates by reference to famous events. For instance, Quraysh used to refer to the Day of the Battle of Fijar, the Fudul compact, the Day of the Arbitration, the death of Hisham ibn al-Mughira, the Year of the Elephant, and the Year of Betrayal during which the tribe of Yarbu' had betrayed the messengers of the Himyarite kings who used to bring the *Kiswa* (cover) to the Ka'ba.

When Islam came, although many important events took place, Quraysh did not use them to specify their dates, since they were related to Islam. There were, for instance, the first revelation of the Qur'an, the *Isra'* and the *Mi'raj*, the journey of the Prophet, may

Allah bless him and grant him peace, to Ta'if, the death of Abu Talib and that of Khadija.

After the *Hijra,* the Muslims used these and subsequent events prior to *Hijra* as a time frame.

The first year of the *Hijra* they called "the Year of Permission," that is, permission to emigrate to Madina.

The second was called "the Year of the Command," a reference to the commandment to take up arms. In this year, the Battle of Badr took place, the believers received the command to fast Ramadan, and the Messenger, may Allah bless him and grant him peace, was ordered to change the direction of the *Qibla.*

The third year was the "Year of Testing": the Battle of Uhud took place and it was a test from Allah to separate the sincere Muslims from the hypocrites.

The fourth year was the "Year of Separation" in which alcohol was prohibited and the tribe of Nadir were expelled from Madina.

Year five was the "Year of the Earthquake" which witnessed the Battles of al-Ahzab or the Confederates, al-Qurayza and Dumat al-Jandal. The incident of the false accusation against 'A'isha also took place at this time.

The sixth year was the "Year of Reconciliation" which saw the Truce of Hudaybiyya and the Ridwan Pledge and also the victory of the Byzantines over Persia in fulfilment of Allah's promise in *Surat ar-Rum* (verses 1-6).

Year seven was called the "Year of Supremacy" which witnessed the war of Khaybar, and when Zaynab, the daughter of al-Harith, gave the poisoned lamb to Allah's Messenger. In this year, the Prophet, may Allah bless him and grant him peace, sent messengers to kings and princes calling them to Islam.

The eighth year was the "Year of the Conquest" or the triumphant return to Makka and the supremacy of Islam. The battle of Hunayn also took place.

Year nine was the "Year of Exemption" (*Bara'a*) because *Surat al-Bara'a* (*at-Tawba*) was revealed. It was also called the "Year of Delegations" as delegations came to Allah's Messenger, may Allah bless him and grant him peace, to announce their acceptance of Islam. The Battle of Tabuk also took place in this year.

Year ten was the "Year of Farewell", during which the Prophet, may Allah bless him and grant him peace, performed his Farewell Pilgrimage, and delivered his famous address on the Day of 'Arafa.

The *Hijra* - the Beginning of Islamic History

After the Messenger of Allah, may Allah bless him and grant him peace, passed away, he left Abu Bakr as-Siddiq, may Allah be pleased with him, as successor. Abu Bakr began his reign by preparing and sending the army of Usama, and then proceeded to fight the apostates and punish them. He collected together the Glorious Qur'an. He was succeeded by 'Umar ibn al-Khattab, may Allah be pleased with him, who established the system of registry and government officials' salaries. He mobilised armies and achieved heroic conquests in Syria, Iraq, Egypt, Persia, and elsewhere.

It is reported that 'Umar ibn al-Khattab once received a letter dated in the month of Sha'ban. He asked the messenger which Sha'ban it was, but the man could not give a definite reply. 'Umar consulted with the Companions for advice. One of them said, "We may use the dating system of the Persians." So they consulted Hurmuzan, a Persian captive, who replied, "We have a dating system," he told them, "which we call *mahruz*, which means 'counting the months (lit. 'month-day')'." They translated this world into Arabic, hence the word '*tarikh*' i.e. dating system.

'Umar said, "Arrange a dating system which the people can use." Someone suggested, "Let us use the Byzantines' calendar system." Another suggested the system followed in Persia. But 'Umar did not like either suggestion. While he was considering the matter, a letter came from Abu Musa al-Ash'ari saying, "We are receiving letters from you undated. Please provide us with a dating system by which we may know the days." So 'Umar said to the Companions, "Why not adopt the *Hijra* as the starting date for the Islamic calendar? It is the most obvious event to use, the most widely agreed upon, and the most firmly connected to Islam and the Muslims." Everyone approved of the suggestion.

Islam Before and After the *Hijra*

When we celebrate the immortal memory of the noble *Hijra* of the Prophet, may Allah bless him and grant him peace, we must call to mind the condition of Islam and its followers before and after it took place. This will allow us to appreciate its value and meaning and the implications which it had for the Muslims. Before the *Hijra,* Islam faced enormous difficulties. The Muslims spared no effort to bring the call of Islam to the hearts and minds of men despite the atmosphere of terror which Quraysh had imposed and the campaigns of torture, violence, and murder which were being waged against the Muslim community. After the *Hijra*, Islam beamed like a light shining out after a long darkness. It became known throughout the world and the Muslims set out to spread its teachings in every place without fear of persecution or murder.

Previously Islam had been a religion of principles, teachings, and rulings without a society in which they could be applied. The society of Quraysh in Makka was dominated by an intolerant paganism which did not allow any individual to apply those principles. The new Muslims therefore concealed their conversion, even from their own parents, brothers and sisters. The Muslims were weak. No one dared perform his religious duties or gather to learn its basic teachings. Most of them went out to the mountains near Makka to pray in secret. Their hearts, however, were full of faith and their souls were sure that Allah would grant them the final triumph.

After the *Hijra*, every Muslim proudly proclaimed his faith. The Muslims became one large family living in and for Islam. They now had mosques in which they could worship Allah and perform their religious duties in freedom and safety, thanks to the support and victory of Almighty Allah.

Earlier, Islam had been confined to the city of Makka and its light was veiled from the outside world. Even within Makka, this light was restricted to a few houses. After the *Hijra*, however, it emanated all over and reached distant places in the East and West.

One of the factors which made the *Hijra* an urgent necessity was the malevolent plan organised by the tyrants of Quraysh to assassinate Allah's Messenger, may Allah bless him and grant him peace. They chose one strong young man from every tribe of Quraysh to collectively stab him, thus preventing his people from taking revenge and obliging them to accept blood money instead. Allah, however, saved him from their treacherous conspiracy. This incident marked the beginning of the flourishing of Islam and its spread through the entire world.

The Messenger's First Address at Madina

As soon as Allah's noble Messenger, may Allah bless him and grant him peace, arrived in Madina, he began the construction of the Great Mosque. He gave a speech calling people to be brothers and to show mutual support, love, kindness and obedience to one another. He warned against polytheism and unbelief. He urged his people not to harbour any hatred against one another or to break their pledges.

A Noble Humanitarian Event

Allah's Messenger, may Allah bless him and grant him peace, established the bond of brotherhood between the Emigrants (*al-Muhajirun*) and the Helpers (*al-Ansar*), saying, "Let every Helper take an Emigrant as his brother." The Helpers welcomed this brotherhood and spared no effort to share everything with the Emigrants: money, food, work. Some of them gave half of their houses to Emigrants or were even willing to relinquish one of their wives for an Emigrant brother to marry after the completion of her waiting period. They all participated in *Jihad* in the path of Allah, achieving miracles as a result of their unity and the perfection of their brotherhood.

41

What Did the Noble *Hijra* Achieve?

The *Hijra* confirmed a number of extremely important facts that should be known and from which we must benefit in order to confront the growing challenges of our time.

It affirmed that truth is victorious no matter how long the journey may be and that falsehood will no doubt be defeated. Injustice, persecution, torture and repression cannot overcome the power of faith once it has become firmly embedded in the hearts of the Muslims.

It affirmed that the idea of one's country has no value, and that remaining in one's land is of no avail, if a citizen has lost his honour and his freedom to practise his religion. Indeed, one's faith is one's homeland. A Muslim is a brother to a Muslim. He does not cheat nor oppress him.

It affirmed the principle of Islamic brotherhood, which is a covenant binding two hearts, a pledge for the sake of a better human existence.

It affirmed that faith is tested by hardships, for these fill the heart with strength and furnish the will with determination so that it never falters, weakens or despairs.

It affirmed that patience, steadfastness, unity and holding fast to the rope of Allah are virtues which bring about miracles and yield the most fruitful results.

Now that we have identified some of the truths that the Noble *Hijra* affirms, can we derive any moral which will assist us in winning our battle against the tyrants of our own time?

Are we linked by brotherhood in Islam, as Allah's Messenger, may Allah bless him and grant him peace, desired? Will we forget our differences and conflicts and stand united, holding together like a well-established building, each part holding the other up? Will we purify our land of intruders and cleanse our lives of falsehood and expel from our intellectual world those materialistic ideologies and destructive principles and rely entirely on the legacy of the Book of Allah and the *Sunna* of His Messenger – and hold fast to them without going astray?

Chapter Six
In the Presence of the Messenger

A man once came to the Prophet, may Allah bless him and grant him peace, and asked him, "When is the Resurrection?"

He replied, "What have you prepared for it?"

"I have not prepared for it any great amount of prayer, fasting or charity," said the man, "However, I love Allah and His Messenger."

The Prophet's response was complete, gentle, and loving: "A man will be with those he loves."

Anas ibn Malik, may Allah be pleased with him, the narrator of this *hadith*, added, "I never saw the Muslims happier about anything – apart from Islam itself – than this statement. "

They had great love for him and gave him their support, thus teaching us the true meaning of love for Allah's Messenger. They were faithful in fulfilling their covenant with Allah and in their love for the Messenger. They declared, *"O our Lord! We have heard a summoner calling to faith, 'Believe in your Lord!' so we believed"* (3:193). They sacrificed their own lives, deeming them cheap, in the path of truth, in submission and humbleness. They lowered their voices before the Messenger. They believed in the Unseen and loved the Messenger of Allah, thus making miracles happen. They preferred the Everlasting Life to this ephemeral world and Divine Guidance to a prosperous life.

It is recorded in a *hadith* on the authority of an-Nasa'i that Allah's Messenger, may Allah bless him and grant him peace, once came out to find some of his Companions sitting together. He asked them, "Why are you sitting together?"

They told him, "We are praying to Allah and praising Him for having guided us to His religion and blessed us with your presence."

He said, "Is that the reason for you staying together?"

They replied, "Yes, indeed."

He said, "My question implied no accusation, but Gabriel came to me and informed me that Almighty Allah is proud of you."

'Umar ibn 'Abdu'l-'Aziz said, "The Messenger of Allah, may Allah bless him and grant him peace, and the governors after him laid down *sunnas* (codes of action). To hold to them is belief in Allah's Book in obedience to Him and strength to practise Allah's religion. No one has the authority to change them or find substitutes for them or to consider any opinion which conflicts with them. Whoever follows them is on the right path and whoever seeks victory through them will be triumphant, whereas those who diverge from them will incur the wrath of Allah and be cast into Hellfire."

Let us reflect on the following verse from the Holy Qur'an:

"If they had only, when they were unjust to themselves, come to you and asked Allah's forgiveness and the Messenger had asked forgiveness for them, they would have found Allah Most Forgiving, Most Merciful." (4:64)

"Whosoever obeys the Messenger has obeyed Allah; and whosoever turns away, We have not sent you as a watcher over them." (4:80)

"Say: If you love Allah, then follow me. Allah will love you and forgive you your sins. And Allah is Forgiving, Merciful." (3:31)

"You have indeed in the Messenger of Allah an excellent example, for him who hopes in Allah and the Last Day and remembers Allah abundantly." (33:21)

These verses command the Muslims to obey and love the Messenger and respect his high status. In the following *hadith*, the Prophet, may Allah bless him and grant him peace, speaks to

'Umar ibn al-Khattab, may Allah be pleased with him. 'Umar said to him, "Truly, Messenger of Allah, you are dearer to me than everything except my own self!"

The Messenger replied, "Nay, I should be dearer to you than your own life."

'Umar declared, "Then truly, by Allah, you are dearer to me than my own life!"

The Messenger then said, "Now you have it, 'Umar! Your faith is complete."

With this clarity and lucidity, Allah's Messenger defined how faith cannot be complete without love for him. In the following *hadith*, the Prophet, may Allah bless him and grant him peace, defines how this love is to be manifested and warns us against any excess in his love. He said, "Do not over-praise me as the Christians over-praised Jesus son of Mary." For the Christians went so far as to deify Jesus and consider him a partner with Allah Almighty. They said, "He is the Son of God" and "the third of three." They also claimed that Allah is Jesus. Thus their love was based on polytheism which corrupted the purity of that love and led them far astray. They over-praised him in a way he himself did not intend. *"It is an appalling word that has emerged from their mouths. They speak only a falsehood."* (18:5)

In the Holy Qur'an, Allah says, *"And when Allah said: 'O Jesus son of Mary! Did you say unto men, Take me and my mother for two gods besides Allah?' He said, 'Glory be to You! It was not for me to say what I had no right to say. Had I said such a thing, You would surely have known it. You know what is in my mind, and I know not what is in Yours. Truly, You, only You, are the All-Knower of all that is hidden and unseen.'"* (5:116)

For this reason, the *hadith* of Allah's Messenger sheds light on the dangers of over-praising him and the implicit polytheism that such an attitude might entail. He has reminded his Companions of the case of the Christians and their Prophet Jesus, peace be upon him.

As for loving the Prophet, may Allah bless him and grant him peace, venerating him, honouring his status and following him, he urged us to do so and showed us the proper manner for doing that.

45

He was the most godfearing. He said, "I am the most godfearing man among you."

One of his prayers was, "O Allah! I ask You to honour me with Your love and the love of those who love You, and the love of every action which brings me closer to Your love! Allah, make my love for You dearer to me than myself and my family and cold water."[1]

In order that our love for him may be positive, effective and fruitful, it must be linked to the appropriate method: *"Say: If you do love Allah, then follow me and Allah will love you."* (3:21) Likewise we should follow his example: *"Indeed in the Messenger of Allah you have a good example to follow."* (33:21)

The Messenger of Allah, may Allah bless him and grant him peace, said, "Follow my *Sunna* and the *Sunna* of the rightly-guided Followers after me. Hold to it firmly. Avoid any innovation (in religion), for every innovation is astray."[2] He also said, "All my nation shall enter Paradise except those who do not want to. Some asked, "Who would not want to?" He said, "Whoever obeys me shall enter Paradise, and whoever disobeys me in fact does not want to (enter Paradise)."[3] Muslim relates on the authority of Anas, may Allah be pleased with him, that the Prophet, may Allah bless him and grant him peace, said, "Whoever abstains from my *Sunna* is not of my nation."

This is the *Sunna* of Allah's Messenger, may Allah bless him and grant him peace, his way of life, and the method which all Muslims should adhere to, after the primary source which is the Holy Qur'an.

Allah, who is Blessed and Exalted, says in *Surat al-Hashr*: *"Whatever the Messenger gives you, take it, and whatever he forbids you, abstain (from it). And fear Allah: truly Allah is severe in punishment"* (59:7).

He also says, in *Surat al-Ahzab*: *"It is not for a believer, man or woman, when Allah and His Messenger have decreed a matter, that they should have any option in their decisions"* (33:36).

---

1. Narrated by at-Tirmidhi in *al-Hilya*, on the authority of Abu'd-Darda'.
2. Narrated by Abu Dawud and at-Tirmidhi.
3. Narrated by al-Bukhari.

Chapter Seven
The Contest of the Lovers

Love of Allah's Messenger, may Allah bless him and grant him peace, is the highest aspiration of any Muslim, in which they compete and which they spare no effort to achieve. No wonder, for Almighty Allah said these words of him: *"Truly, you are of a tremendous character."* (68:40) He sent him as a mercy to mankind. He cares deeply about his nation. He is benevolent and merciful to them. About such attributes, Allah Almighty says: *"It grieves him that you should receive any injury or difficulty. He is anxious over you, for the believers he is full of pity, kind and merciful."* (9:128)

Allah Almighty commanded us to send blessings and peace on him. He started with Himself, then His angels, then addressed the command to us: *"Allah Almighty and His angels send blessings on him so greet him with all respect"* (33:56). Likewise, Allah Almighty commanded us to venerate him and hold him in high esteem: *"Those who believe in him, honour him, help him, and follow the Light which is sent down with him, it is they who will prosper"* (7:157). It is reported that when these verses were revealed, Abu Bakr and 'Umar ibn al-Khattab never raised their voices in the presence of the Prophet, may Allah bless him and grant him peace. They would speak as if whispering.

Almighty Allah says: *"O you who believe! Put not yourselves forward before Allah and His Messenger."* (49:2)

He also says: *"O you who believe! Raise not your voices above the voice of the Prophet."* (49:2) Likewise: *"Deem not the summons of the Messenger among yourselves like the summons of one of you to another."* (24:63)

It is narrated that 'Amr ibn al-'As said, "No one was dearer to me and greater in my sight than Allah's Messenger, may Allah bless him and grant him peace. I could hardly look directly at his face out of respect for him. Were I asked to describe him, I would not be able to, since I never filled my eyes with his sight."

At-Tirmidhi narrates on the authority of Anas that Allah's Messenger, may Allah bless him and grant him peace, used to go out to his Companions, both Emigrants and Helpers, while they were seated in the company of Abu Bakr and 'Umar. They would look at him, and he would look at them, and they would smile at him and he would smile at them.

Abu Ibrahim at-Tajibi said, "It is an obligation upon every believer, whenever he mentions him or hears him mentioned, to be humble and reverent, to show respect and to refrain from movement, feeling awe and veneration for him just as he would if he were actually present before him."

Once the Caliph Abu Ja'far had a debate with Imam Malik in the mosque of Allah's Messenger, may Allah bless him and grant him peace. Imam Malik said, "O Commander of the Faithful! Do not raise your voice in this mosque, for Allah the Exalted has Himself shown the proper manner to address him in the following verse: 'Do not lift up your voices above the voice of the Prophet' 929:3). He praised some people for their respect: 'Those who lower their voices in the presence of Allah's Messenger' (49:3), and blamed others, 'Those who call to you from behind the private rooms, most of them do not know' (49:4)." Imam Malik continued, "and he is worthy of respect in his death just as he was in life." At this Abu Ja'far calmed down and lowered his voice.

Mus'ab ibn 'Abdullah said, "When the Prophet, may Allah bless him and grant him peace, was mentioned in the presence of Imam Malik, his colour would change and he would lower his head. This distressed the people with him so they asked him about it one day. He told them, 'Had you seen what I have seen, you would not have disapproved of my behaviour. I have seen Muhammad ibn al-Munkadir (the master of the Qur'an reciters) who used to shed tears as soon as we asked him about a *hadith*.

We would stop asking him out of pity for him. I also used to see Ja'far ibn Muhammad, who was known for his constant prayer and his smiling face, and when he heard the Prophet, may Allah bless him and grant him peace, mentioned, he would become pale. Never had I seen him narrating a *hadith* by Allah's Messenger without being in a state of *wudu'* (ablution).'"

Descriptions of Allah's Messenger, may Allah bless him and grant him peace, are found in the revealed Books in various contexts. Ahmad ibn 'Ata' ibn Yasar once said, "I met 'Abdullah ibn 'Amr ibn al-'As, may Allah be pleased with him, and said to him, 'Tell me how Allah's Messenger was described in the Torah.' He replied, 'He is certainly described there, just as he is in the Qur'an. It says, "O Prophet, We have sent you as a witness and a bearer of good tidings and a warner, and a protection for the unlettered. You are My servant and Messenger whom I have named the Trusting. You are neither harsh nor stern, nor given to strutting in the marketplaces. You do not repay evil with evil. Instead you forgive and pardon. Allah shall not bring you to Himself until the wrong religion is made straight, when people say, 'There is no deity but Allah.' Thus the blind eyes shall see and deaf ears shall hear and veiled hearts shall be opened."'"

Wahb ibn Munabbih mentions that Allah Almighty said to David in the Psalms: "O David! There shall come after you a Prophet whose name shall be Ahmad and Muhammad. He shall be truthful and a master. He shall never incur My wrath. I have forgiven him his former and later sins. His nation is worthy of My mercy. I have granted them optional acts of devotion similar to those which I gave the Prophets and have imposed upon them the obligations which I imposed upon the Prophets and the Messengers. They shall come to Me on the Day of Judgement with their light like the Prophets themselves . . . O David! I have preferred Muhammad and his nation over all nations."

On the authority of Sa'id ibn Abi Hilal, 'Abdullah ibn 'Amr once said to Ka'b, "Tell me about the description of Muhammad and his nation!" He answered, "I find them mentioned in the Book of Allah Almighty: 'Verily, Ahmad and his nation give thanks constantly, thanking Allah Almighty for every good thing and evil thing, glorifying Him in every high place, extolling Him wherever they are. Their cry is in the heaven. When praying, they have a sound like that of bees. Like the angels, they pray in rows, and they fight in rows as they stand in prayer. When they wage war for the sake of Allah, the angels are before them and behind them with strong lances. When they attend to fight, Allah shades them (and he gestured with his hand) as the eagles shade their nests. Never do they retreat from the attack.'"

He quotes it again with another chain of authorities going as far back as Ka'b, which runs as follows:

"His nation are the praisers. They praise Allah under all conditions and glorify Him everywhere. They follow the movement of the sun,[1] for they offer five prayers at fixed times, even on a slippery rock. They wear wrappers around their waists, and wash their limbs." He also quotes it in an extended version with another chain going back to Ka'b.[2]

Ya'qub ibn Sufyan al-Fasawi al-Hafiz narrates on the authority of al-Hasan ibn 'Ali, may Allah be pleased with him, "I once asked my uncle Hind ibn Abi Hala about the speech of the Messenger of Allah, may Allah bless him and grant him peace. He said:

'Allah's Messenger, may Allah bless him and grant him peace, was constantly sad, and always deep in thought. He had no rest and would not speak unless it was necessary. He was silent for long periods and would speak distinctly. His words would be comprehensive and his discourse was decisive (that is, his sentences were distinctly separated from each other, so that if someone wanted to count his words, they could have done so). He never spoke superfluous or insufficient words, and his speech was soft (that is, his character was gentle and easy-going), never harsh or humiliating. He would value Allah's blessings, even when these were few, and would never criticise any of them.

'Nothing could withstand his wrath when the Truth was opposed until he had given victory to the Truth. (Another version reads: "The world, and that which pertains to it, could not anger

---

1. That is, they watch the sun in order to know the time for their prayers.
2. Muhammad Yusuf Kandalawi, *Hayat as-Sahaba*, dated 1317 AH.]

him, but if Truth was opposed, nothing could stand in his way until he had given victory to the Truth.") He would not get angry for his own sake or seek victory for himself. When he gestured, he would do so with his entire hand and when he was pleased he would turn his palm upside down. When he spoke he would place his left thumb against the palm of his right hand. When angry, he would turn away firmly, whereas when he rejoiced he would look down. Most of his merriment took the form of a smile. He would smile even at a cool breeze.'"

Al-Hasan said, "I hid this from al-Husayn ibn 'Ali for a time, and then told it to him and discovered that he had already heard it. I asked him about the subject which I had enquired about and found that he had asked his father about the way he used to enter and leave, and to sit down and about his appearance, and he had not neglected any detail."

Al-Husayn said, "I once asked my father about how Allah's Messenger used to be at home and he replied:

'When he entered his own home, it was only by permission. When he entered, he would divide his time into three parts: one for Allah, one for his family, and one for himself. For the time allocated for himself, he would sit with people, both the common and the elite, withholding nothing from them. He used to say to them, "Let those who are present inform those who are absent. Tell me of the needs of those who cannot come themselves, for truly whosoever informs a ruler about the need of someone who cannot do it himself, Allah will give him steadfastness on the Day of Judgement.'"

"I asked him about the Prophet's behaviour when he was outside and he said:

'Allah's Messenger, may Allah bless him and grant him peace, used to remain silent except in those matters which were his concern. He would make people feel relaxed and never repel them. He would give the people of status their due honour and give them authority over others. He used to be aware of people, always on his guard against them, without refraining from smiling at them or being discourteous. He was always concerned about his Companions' affairs and used to ask people about their needs. He praised what was good and encouraged it and checked what was bad until it was inhibited and finally removed. His instructions were moderate and never contradictory. He was never caught unawares lest others should be oblivious to truth or swerve from it. He was prepared for every eventuality and would neither fall short of what was right nor overstep it. Those people who were nearest to him were the best of people, and better still in his sight were those whose counsel was given to people at large. The dearest of them to him were those who were the most ready to help and provide assistance.'

"I asked him about the way he sat. He said:

'Whenever he sat or stood up, he would mention the Name of Allah. He would sit in various places and forbid people from always sitting in the same place. When he came to a group of people he would take a place like anyone else, without any prominence, and would tell other people to also follow this practice. He would give every one of his Companions in the assembly his due respect. Everybody believed that no one had received more hospitality than he himself. Whenever someone sat or stood with him to ask him a question, he would stay with him patiently until the person asking would depart. Whoever asked him for something would leave with his need satisfied or with some gentle words. People loved him and his character and he became like a father to them. They were all equal to him when truth was in question.

'His gatherings were marked by leniency, modesty, patience and trust. Voices were never raised, no blasphemies were uttered, and no one's faults were published. People were all equal, distinguished from one another only by piety. They were always humble, respected the old, and were kind to the young. They gave preference to those with needs and to protecting strangers.'

"When I asked him about his silence, he replied:

'He was silent at four times: out of mild gentleness, in caution, when evaluating a matter or listening to people, and in meditation on this transient life and things that we have to endure. He combined both gentleness and patience. He was never angered or provoked by anything. In his caution, he would always hold to what was best, and would constantly uphold that which brought people the good of this world and the next.'"

Chapter Eight
Muhammad as Seen by
Unbiased Western Thinkers

Ever since the advent of Islam, unbiased Western thinkers have focused on the personality of Muhammad, may Allah bless him and grant him peace, and studied the various characteristics that Allah bestowed upon him. The following are examples:

Thomas Carlyle

One of these unbiased thinkers was the English writer, Thomas Carlyle, who was impressed by the "heroism" manifested by great men. He studied the heroes' lives and wrote a book called *Heroes* in which he devoted an entire chapter to the Prophet of Islam. He warned his readers not to believe the falsehoods and widespread distortions about Islam and its Prophet. He said that "for fourteen centuries, the message brought by Muhammad has remained a source of guidance for many millions. Is it possible, then, that this message, for which millions have lived and died, could be a lie or a deceit? ... Has anyone seen a liar able to create a religion, and spread it as with the case of Islam? ... The message of Muhammad was nothing but truth and honesty - it was a true inspiration, a light for humanity as a whole. This was by Allah's command, and *'That is Allah's blessings, which He gives to whomsoever He will.'*"

He then goes on to speak specifically about the Messenger: "I have admired Muhammad because he was free from hypocrisy, boastfulness, pretension, or greed for worldly things. He was unique in the greatness of his soul, and with the Creator of the universe and its creatures. He saw the secret of existence open in front of him."

"The voice of Mohammad came from the heart of the desert, pure and undefiled; it penetrated the hearts, and became firmly rooted. Mohammad was neither arrogant nor lowly; he rejected the prevailing conditions and did not fear the false, vain illusions. From his humble position and patched dress, he addressed kings and rulers, guiding them to truth, and did not accept money, status or authority. He lived as an ascetic, striving for the sake of Allah, working for the spread of his religion, indifferent to the obstacles on the way, until the true religion of Allah became victorious, and it spread and flourished."

Lord Headley

Lord Headley is another writer who studied Islam and was fair to the noble Prophet. He wrote, "I thought and prayed for forty years to come to the truth. I must confess that my visit to the Muslim East filled me with respect for the Mohammadan faith in its simplicity and ease, which requires man to worship Allah throughout his life, not just on Sundays. I thank Allah for having guided me to Islam, which has become firmly rooted in my heart and has made me happier and calmer than ever before. I had been in the darkness of ignorance and Islam brought me out to the light of knowledge."

Lord Headley speaks of the personality of Muhammad ibn 'Abdullah, may Allah bless him and grant him peace, as the highest ideal: "The Arabian Prophet possessed the most distinguished morals, and a personality which developed to its perfect best throughout every step of his life. We are in great need of a perfect model which will satisfy our needs in this life and the personality of Mohammad, the Holy Prophet, fulfils that need. For he is the mirror which reflects high understanding, generosity, nobility, and courage, bravery, patience and forbearance, gentleness, forgiveness and modesty, and all the essential characteristics which enhance human life to its highest perfection."

Michael Hart

Michael Hart is a well-known astrophysicist. He has an interest in heroism and great historical figures. He has published a book called *The One Hundred Greatest Men. Their Greatest is Mohammad, the Messenger of Allah.* Hart is not a Muslim. He is an American Christian researcher.

He chose one hundred personalities who left a great impact on the history of mankind. His choice of Muhammad, may Allah bless him and grant him peace, as the greatest is undoubtedly an acknowledgement by the West of the Prophet's unsurpassed excellence and the favours of Islam on human civilisation.

He writes: "Mohammad was the only man in history who achieved absolute success in both religious and worldly affairs. He called to Islam and spread it as one of the greatest religions. He also established himself as a political, military and spiritual leader. Despite the passage of fourteen hundred years, his influence remains ever-active.

"With those who believed in his message, he succeeded in establishing a vast empire which extended from the borders of India to the Atlantic Ocean. History has seen no greater empire. They propagated Islam in every land they entered and the Prophet Mohammad was the first and only man responsible for the establishment of the foundations of Islam and the Shari'ah law, together with the norms of social and moral behaviour and codes of dealings among people in their religious life. Similarly, the Qur'an, which was revealed to him alone, provided the Muslims with all they needed for their lives in this world and in the hereafter."

Dr Girnieu

Dr. Girnieu writes about the reasons for his conversion with great happiness: "I read the verses relevant to medical and natural sciences, and studied them. I then compared them to the medical and natural data which I had studied at the university. I found that the verses of the Qur'an were exactly consistent with them. I became a Muslim because I had a firm conviction that Muhammad, may Allah bless him and grant him peace, had brought the clear truth more than a thousand years before we knew it in our modern age. I am confident that if any technician or scientist compared what is revealed in the Holy Qur'an with the facts known to his discipline - as I myself did - he would certainly join Islam like myself unless he is obstinate, or there is some sickness in his heart."

René Guénon

Guénon – or 'Abdu'l-Wahid Yahya as he called himself after he became Muslim – writes: "I wanted to find a divine text to which I could hold, which had never been subject to any corruption. I could not find anything, after a long and exhaustive search, other than the Holy Qur'an. It was the only text which convinced me and fulfilled the need which was in my heart. The Prophet of Islam was the Prophet I loved, under whose banner I could happily march. His sayings and acts filled me with happiness and spiritual tranquillity. But for him, humanity would have drowned in materialism, atheism, immorality, and spiritual backwardness."

About Islamic culture and its impact on the West, he says: "Islamic culture and science were the source of enlightenment and guidance. If it were not for the scientists and philosophers of Islam, the West would have continued to wander blindly in the darkness of ignorance."

Alphonse Dinet

Alphonse Dinet was an international painter who embraced Islam after years of meditation and thought. He took the name Nasir ad-Din – Religion's supporter – and proved indeed to be so.

He spared no effort to defend Allah's religion by rectifying the fallacies and distortions about the truth of Islam spread by Orientalists. He wrote a biography of the Prophet, may Allah bless him and grant him peace, which he dedicated to the souls of the martyrs who had died in the Great War. "The Muhammadan doctrine," he wrote, "is no barrier to thinking. A man can be a full Muslim and remain a free thinker at the same time."

"Allah in Islam does not take the shape of a human or any other form. Yahweh, the God of the Jews, whom they worship as the very essence of purity, is manifested in a debased and humble form. Allah is portrayed in the same way in the corrupted text of the Gospels. In Islam, however, Allah is spoken of by the Qur'an and the Messenger, and no painter's brush or sculptor's chisel has had the audacity to try and portray Him. For Allah, the Glorious and Exalted, has no form, no limits and nothing is like Him." *"He is the One, the Unique, the Self-Sufficient. He begets not nor was He begotten, and there is none like unto Him"* (112:1-4).

Tolstoy

Tolstoy, the great Russian novelist, was grieved to see the enemies of Islam launching their offensive distortions against it and against its noble Prophet. "Without doubt," he writes, "this Prophet was one of the greatest of all reformers who have rendered incomparable services to humanity. It should be sufficient to point out that he guided his entire community to the light of the Truth and made them incline towards peace and stop bloodshed. It is enough honour for him to have opened the door to progress, a mighty achievement which could only have been accomplished by an individual who was given superhuman strength, wisdom and knowledge. For all these reasons, he is worthy of our esteem, our respect, and our admiration."

Roger Garaudy

Garaudy, the French Socialist and Marxist philosopher and sociologist, an ex-member of the French Parliament, was blessed with Islam after a lifetime's study of different religions, ideologies and beliefs. When he turned his attention to Islam and came to understand its true nature, he rejected all else and proclaimed that he could no longer remain silent. Affirming that Islam was the true religion and the only means of saving mankind from the darkness of ignorance, which is in fact the outcome of their false faiths and erroneous ideologies, he speaks at length about Islam and the future of Islam: "The civilisation of the future stems from Islam, both as a doctrine and as a way of life."

He speaks about the tolerance of Islam: "The Qur'an recognised the People of the Book – the followers of the Torah and the Gospels – and gave them the freedom to choose between their religions and the religion of Islam. The Prophet Muhammad, may Allah bless him and grant him peace, stated: 'No Arab is better than a non-Arab, except by fear of Allah.'"

"In Islam, therefore, people are distinguished from each other by fear of Allah and good conduct, not by wealth, status or lineage. All are equal before Allah. There are no class prejudices, no chosen peoples, no privileged races. Islam is the faith of brotherhood, social solidarity, and equality in their best forms. Islam had no need of power or weapons to spread, since its nature, its laws, its tolerance, and the good example which its Messenger exemplified, had already found their way to people's hearts."

Garaudy then mentions the *hadith* of the Prophet, may Allah bless him and grant him peace: "We have returned from the minor *Jihad* to the greater *Jihad*"; the *Jihad* against the whims and desires of the *nafs*, the ego, and the tendencies which it harbours such as injustice, jealousy, greed, weakness, and the love of money. He then points out: "This great teaching of the Prophet, may Allah bless him and grant him peace, is an important lesson for those revolutionaries who would change all and everything – except themselves."

Garaudy cites a number of *hadiths*, explaining the beauty and exalted humanness which they exemplify. He devotes particular attention to the following *hadiths*: "None of you is a true believer until he loves for his brother what he loves for himself," and "A Muslim is a brother to another Muslim. He does not wrong or cheat him or lie to him or despise him," and "Believers are like a building, each brick supporting the next." Garaudy then states: "These *hadiths* form a comprehensive constitution which Muslims should adhere to in their lives, as a nation possessing noble objectives based on sound principles. It is a constitution which protects their rights among themselves and endeavours to establish a true friendship which strengthens the relations of believers with one another and makes them truly one building, each part supporting the others."

Bosworth Smith

In 1874, Bosworth Smith, a professor at Oxford, delivered a lecture entitled "Mohammed and Mohammedanism" in which he said: "In the writings of the early historians who addressed the subject of Mohammed and his message we find no legends, fantasies or impossible events. Everything is crystal-clear, as though the rays of the morning sun had revealed everything. It is astonishing that there is no personality in history about whom so much has been written as Muhammad, the Messenger of Allah."

David Margoliouth

In his book, *Mohammed*, published in 1905 as a volume in the *Great Men of History* series, David Margoliouth wrote: "It is impossible to enumerate all those who have written on the life of Mohammed. They consider it a mark of honourable distinction to have their names among those who have written about the life of this Messenger."

The magazine, *al-Muqtabas*, which used to be edited by Muhammad Kurd 'Ali about eighty years ago, stated that the number of books on the biography of the Prophet published in European languages had reached 1300 books. This does not include what was published during the last eighty years in different languages nor the many biographies written in Arabic.

Conclusion

This book is a humble contribution to the noble *Sira* of the Prophet Muhammad, may Allah bless him and grant him peace, which I wanted to present to our children in the hope that the *Sira* will become an illuminating light for them, incarnating for them the ideal example of the Prophet, may Allah bless him and grant him peace. For he was the highest model for all humanity. He was the guide, by Allah's leave, to the Straight Path. Allah the Exalted says: *"Truly, you guide to a Straight Path"* (42:52).

Inasmuch as we teach our children to love him and to hold fast to the objectives of his *Shari'a* and to emulate his character, we will grow closer and closer to the true springs of Islam and of its tolerant *Shari'a*. This is because faith begins with love and grows stronger through love until it reaches the summit of perfection. He, upon whom be peace, said: "You will not reach perfect faith until Allah and His Messenger are more beloved to you than all else." True love can be manifested only in the implementation of his *Shari'a*, which was represented in the personality of the noble Messenger who embodied the eternal Divine Constitution of Islam, which Allah the Exalted revealed to his heart and commanded him to make plain to all people.

He was worthy of being addressed by his Lord who educated him in this way: *"Truly, you are of a tremendous character."* (68:4). Certainly, his character was tremendous for he was the embodiment of the Qur'an. In all situations – in distress or when at ease, with those he loved or those he hated, in private or in public, at war or in peace – the Chosen One, may Allah bless him and grant him peace, acted according to the principles of the Qur'an, as he was described by the Lady 'A'isha, may Allah be pleased with her. He came to teach humanity how to lead life in accordance with the pattern prescribed by Allah.

This book is but a brief survey of some of those situations. Perhaps we may implant them in the souls of our children and deepen their love for them and place them as examples before their eyes. Our children should only be impressed by the "tremendous character" and the unique qualities and perfect example of "the Mercy Bestowed", may Allah bless him and grant him peace.

Let us choose a further incident or two from the life of this man of tremendous character.

Remind your children that unlike all the great events that history witnessed, the life of the Prophet, may Allah bless him and grant him peace, drives home morals and lessons of incomparable value. He was persecuted by the people of Makka, but he later returned to them as a triumphant conqueror. Did his overwhelming victory render him arrogant or tyrannical? Did force and power render him a dictator? What did he do with the people who had persecuted him and his followers? He said to them, "Go, you are free."

This was the most thought-provoking of all events. Gabriel came with the Angel of the Mountains while the Prophet was suffering most grievously from Quraysh. The Angel stood and waited for one simple signal from the Prophet and he was ready to crash the mountains down upon them and put an end to the persecutors, in revenge for what they had done to the Prophet and his Companions.

What did the Messenger, may Allah bless him and grant him peace, do? Did he think of vengeance against those who had persecuted him and his family and his followers, those who stood in the way of his call by which he was bringing people from darkness into light? No, he did not! His response was very telling of his great character.

He said: "I hope that Allah will bring forth from their descendants those who will worship Allah alone, and not associate partners with Him."

May Allah bless you and grant you peace, O my master, O Messenger of Allah! May Allah bless you and grant you peace, O you who are the Mercy bestowed unto all nations!

Fathers! Educators! Teach the story of his life to your children! Teach them of these great events! Teach them about his tremendous character! Teach them how our master Muhammad was appointed Allah's perfect vice-regent!

Many of our offspring have fallen prey to the snares of the West, lured by their attractive appearance which has conquered their hearts. Consequently, their souls are divided between various philosophies and ideologies. We, the fathers and educators, have failed to implant in their hearts the glory of the Muhammadan *Sira* and have not drawn their attention to the examples and lessons which it contains. Our young people are in the direst need of this treasure which we have buried with our own hands. Thus, our children are ignorant of its value.

"A man is the enemy of what he does not know."

Let us teach our children to love him and to love his noble family and to love his rightly-guided Companions.

Allah the Exalted says: *"Say: If you love Allah, then follow me, Allah will love you."*

O Lord Allah! Teach us to love him well, and to love his Family and Companions, who are the most honourable of mankind, and those who follow them with excellence until the Day of Judgement! Render us steadfast in true love, until we come to him and find him pleased with us, so that we may drink from the Basin from his two noble hands together with those that You have blessed among the Prophets, the Saints, the Martyrs and the Righteous.

May Allah bless the noblest of all Messengers, the master of the first and the last, our master Muhammad ibn 'Abdullah, the unlettered Prophet, the guide to the Straight Path, the Path of Allah, in Whose dominion is the heavens and the earth and what is between! Amen!

And our last prayer is: Praise is for Allah, the Lord of the worlds!

Bibliography of Works Cited

The Glorious Qur'an

Abu Hurayra fi daw' arwiyyatih. MA thesis.

Al-Aghani, Abu'l-Faraj al-Isfahani.

'Azim qadruhu wa' kanatuhu 'inda rabbihi 'azza wa jall, Dr. Khalil Ibrahim Mulla Khatir.

Dhu'n-Nurayn, 'Uthman ibn 'Affan, al-'Aqqad.

Dirasat tarikhiyya.

Hawl al-Ihtifal bi' l-Mawlid an-Nabawi, Dr. Muhammad 'Alawi al-Maliki.

Al-Hawi li' l-fatawi, Imam as-Suyuti.

Hayat Muhammad, Muhammad Husayn Haykal.

Hayat as-Sahaba, Muhammad Yusuf Kandhalavi.

al-Hilya, Abu Nu'aym.

Hujjat Allah al-Baligha, Wali Allah ad-Dihlawi.

Hijjat al-Wada' wa-juz' 'umarat an-Nabi, Shaykh Muhammad Zakariyya Kandhalavi.

al-Isaba fi tamyiz as-Sahaba, Ibn Hajar.

al-Isti'ab fi ma'rifat al-Ashab, Ibn 'Abd al-Barr

al-Jami' as-Sahih, Imam al-Bukhari.

al-Jami' as-Sahih, Imam Muslim.

Jawahir as-Sira an-Nabawiyya, Ibn Hazm al-Andalusi.

Khatam an-Nabiyyin, Muhammad Abu Zahra.

al-Kamil, Ibn al-Athir.

al-Mawahib al-Ladunniyya, az-Zarqani.

Al-Muhabbar, Ibn Habib.

al-Musnad, Imam Ahmad ibn Hanbal.

al-Mustadrak, Al-Hakim.

Nahj al-Burda, Ahmad Shawqi.

Risala fi tarikh al-'Arab, Caussin de Perceval.

ar-Rasul al-Qa'id, Mahmud Shith Khattab.

ar-Rawd al-Unuf, Imam as-Suhayli.

ar-Risala al-Muhammadiyya, Abu'l-Hasan an-Nadwi.

Riyad as-Salihin, Imam an-Nawawi.

Sharh al-Kirmani 'ala Sahih al-Bukhari.

ash-Shifa', al-Qadi 'Iyad.

as-Sira an-Nabawiyya, Ibn Hisham.

as-Sira an-Nabawiyya, Abu'l-Hasan an-Nadwi.

as-Sira al-Halabiyya, 'Ali ibn Burhan ad-Din al-Halabi.

Subul al-Huda wa'r-rashad, Imam Muhammad Yusuf as-Salihi.

Sunan, Abu Dawud.

Sunan, Ibn Maja

Sunan, at-Tirmidhi.

at-Tabaqat, Ibn Sa'd.

Tafsir, Ibn Kathir

Tafsir, at-Tabari

Tarajim Sayyidat bayt an-Nubuwwa, 'A'isha 'Abdu'r-Rahman (Bint Shati')

'Uyun al-athar fi sirat Sayyid al-Bashar, Muhammad ibn Muhammad ibn Sayyid an-Nas.